Stopwatch

Teacher's Guide

5

Geraldine D. Geniusas

Richmond

Richmond

58 St Aldates
Oxford
OX1 1ST
United Kingdom

Stopwatch Teacher's Guide Level 5

First Edition: September 2016
First Reprint: January 2018
ISBN: 978-607-06-1375-3

© Text: Geraldine D. Geniusas
© Richmond Publishing, S.A. de C.V. 2016
Av. Río Mixcoac No. 274, Col. Acacias,
Del. Benito Juárez, C.P. 03240, Ciudad de México

Publisher: Justine Piekarowicz
Editorial Team: Gabriela Pérez
Design Team: Jaime Angeles, Daniel Mejía
Pre-Press Coordinator: Daniel Santillán
Pre-Press Team: Susana Alcántara, Virginia Arroyo, Daniel Santillán
Cover Design: Karla Avila
Cover Photograph: © **Shutterstock** Ivan Smuk (Rowers in eight-oar rowing boats on the tranquil lake)

All rights reserved. No part of this work may be reproduced, stored in a retrieval system or transmitted in any form or by any means without prior written permission from the Publisher.

Richmond publications may contain links to third party websites or apps. We have no control over the content of these websites or apps, which may change frequently, and we are not responsible for the content or the way it may be used with our materials. Teachers and students are advised to exercise discretion when accessing the links.

The Publisher has made every effort to trace the owner of copyright material; however, the Publisher will correct any involuntary omission at the earliest opportunity.

Printed in Mexico by   COMERCIALIZADORA DE IMPRESOS OM S.A. de C.V.
Álvaro Obregón, Ciudad de México, Insurgentes Sur 1889 Piso 12 Col. Florida.
In January 2018

Contents

- 4   Scope and Sequence
- 6   Introduction to the Teacher's Guide
- 10   **Unit 0**   Why do we learn English?
- 15   **Unit 1**   How does music affect you?
- 29   **Unit 2**   What have you done so far?
- 43   **Unit 3**   How do you help at home?
- 57   **Unit 4**   Are you lucky?
- 71   **Unit 5**   Where would you rather go?
- 85   **Unit 6**   Why do we behave the way we do?
- 99   **Unit 7**   What's it like in your country?
- 113   **Unit 8**   What's your dream job?
- 126   CD1 and CD2 Contents
- 127   Verb List

Scope and Sequence

Unit	Vocabulary	Grammar	Skills
0 **Why do we learn English?**	**Review:** aches and pains, habits, travel abroad	Present continuous; (future meaning) First conditional; Past simple and past continuous; Might, would; Should	**Listening:** Identifying specific information
1 **How does music affect you?**	**Music:** classical, country, jazz, Latin, pop, rap, reggae, rock, world music **Adjectives:** catchy, dramatic, inspiring, loud, moving, relaxing	Comparatives; Gerunds	**Listening:** Predicting meaning from pictures **Speaking:** Describing songs and feelings **Project:** Making a playlist
2 **What have you done so far?**	**Life Experiences:** camp overnight, change your look, design your own web page, learn to play a musical instrument, ride a horse, sail a boat, perform in a play, travel by plane	Present perfect; *For, how long, since*	**Writing:** Identifying signpost words in writing **Speaking:** Using signpost words in speaking **Project:** Making a board game with life experiences
3 **How do you help at home?**	**The Household:** cupboard, drawer, garbage, laundry, living room, tablecloth, trash, yard **Phrasal Verbs:** clean out, hang up, pick up, put away, take out, throw away, wash up, wipe off	Past perfect	**Listening:** Identifying specific information **Speaking:** Describing a household chores wheel **Project:** Performing a play about household chores
4 **Are you lucky?**	**Lucky Charms:** evil eye, fortune cat, fortune cookies, four-leaf clover, horse shoe, ladybug, rabbit's foot **Adverbs of Manner:** accidentally, badly, cleverly, deliberately, noisily, quickly, silently, slowly, stupidly, well	Second conditional	**Reading:** Identifying the author's audience and tone **Writing:** Writing to a specific audience and giving advice **Project:** Making a *Superstitions around the world* poster

Unit	Vocabulary	Grammar	Skills
5 **Where would you rather go?**	**Air Travel:** boarding pass, booking a flight, customs, luggage, passport, visa stamp **Human-made Wonders:** Angkor Wat, Colosseum, Blue Mosque, Machu Picchu, Great Wall of China, Moai statues, Ponte Vecchio, Pyramid of Giza	Preferences; Intensifiers; *Too, Enough*	**Listening:** Inferring relationships between events **Writing:** Using past forms to write a narrative **Project:** Making a traveler's guide
6 **Why do we behave the way we do?**	**Phrasal Verbs:** break up, figure out, get along, get over, give up, go on, keep it to yourself, turn in, own up, tell on someone	Could; May; Might	**Reading:** Reading moral dilemmas **Writing:** Using transition words for contradiction to write a solution to a moral dilemma **Project:** Debating about social media
7 **What's it like in your country?**	**Food Around the World:** Acarajé, Baklava, British lunch, Ceviche, Dim Sum, Goulash, Tandoori chicken **Cooking Verbs:** baking, boiling, frying, grilling, roasting, steaming **Adjectives:** bland, chewy, crispy, raw, sour, spicy, sticky	The passive; Present and past	**Listening:** Identifying supporting information **Writing:** Using correct capitalization and punctuation **Project:** Writing a recipe for a popular dish
8 **What's your dream job?**	**Unusual Jobs:** animation director, chef, sports coach, computer game programmer, crime scene investigator, graffiti artist, marine biologist, travel writer	Relative clauses; Defining, non-defining; *That, which, who*	**Reading:** Reading a magazine article **Writing:** Writing a summary **Project:** Organizing a tribe

The Concept

Stopwatch is a motivating, six-level secondary series built around the concept of visual literacy.

- *Stopwatch* constructs students' language skills from A0 to B1 of the Common European Framework of Reference (CEFR).
- A stopwatch symbolizes energy, speed, movement and competition and gives immediate feedback. The *Stopwatch* series offers dynamic, engaging activities and timed challenges that encourage students to focus and train for mastery.
- *Stopwatch* has a strong visual component to facilitate and deepen learning through authentic tasks, compelling images and the use of icons.
- The series was conceived for the international market, with a wide range of topics, incorporating cultures from around the world.
- The six-level framework of the series allows for different entry points to fit the needs of each school or group of students.
- The syllabus has been carefully structured. Each level recycles and expands on the language that was used in the previous books. This process of spiraled language development helps students internalize what they are learning.
- Each level of *Stopwatch* covers 90 – 120 hours of classroom instruction, plus an additional 20 hours of supplementary activities and materials in the Teacher's Guide and Teacher's Toolkit.

Student's Book & Workbook

Units are divided into distinct spreads, each with a clear focus:

- A **Big Question** establishes the central theme of the unit and promotes critical thinking, curiosity and interest in learning.
- **Vocabulary** is presented in thematic sets and with rich visual support to convey meaning.
- **Grammar** is introduced in context, enabling students to see the meaning, form and use of the structure.
- **Skills** (reading, listening, writing and speaking) are developed through engaging topics.
- **Culture** invites the learner to immerse oneself in the rich variety of cultures and peoples on our planet.
- **Review** activities provide consolidated practice for each of the grammar and vocabulary areas.
- In the **Project**, students apply the skills they learned in the unit to a creative task built around the Big Question.
- **Just for Fun** is a page with fun activities that teachers can assign to fast finishers.
- The **Workbook** pages offer extended practice with the vocabulary, structures and skills of the unit.
- **The Student's CD** contains all the listening material in the units.

Teacher's Guide

Brief instructions or summaries provide a quick guide for each Student's Book activity, including **answer keys** and **audio scripts**.

A fun and engaging **warm-up** activity reviews previous knowledge and prepares students for what will be seen in each lesson.

A **wrap-up** task practices newly-learned material. Warm-ups and wrap-ups usually take the form of games.

Extension tasks promote use of language in communication and real-life situations.

Digital options provide alternatives to the projects using electronic media.

Specific questions, related to the Big Question of the unit, stimulate critical thinking.

Teaching tips help develop and enrich teachers' skills.

Teacher's Toolkit (printable materials)

The Teacher's Toolkit is a comprehensive resource that is delivered in two CDs.

CD1 includes the Class Audio and Worksheets

Worksheets
- Grammar Worksheets (2 per unit) with Answer Key
- Reading Worksheets (2 per unit) with Guidelines and Answer Key
- Vocabulary Worksheets (2 per unit) with Answer Key

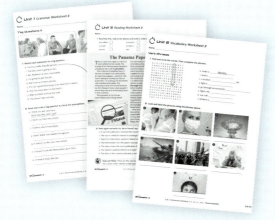

CD2 includes Project Rubrics, Score Cards, Tests and Test Audios

Project Rubrics
- These contain proposed criteria that can be used to evaluate students' performance in the completion of the unit projects.

Scorecard
- These help students evaluate their progress by reflecting on their newly-acquired grammar, vocabulary, reading and listening skills.

Tests

- **Placement Tests** (Beginner & Intermediate) with Grading Scale and Answer Key
These will help teachers assess students' level of English on an individual and group basis and select appropriate tests.

- **Standard Tests** (1 per unit) with Answer Key
These cover the vocabulary and grammar from the units, as well as reading and listening skills.
- **Tests Plus** (1 per unit) with Answer Key
These are the **extended** version of the Standard Tests, which include an additional communication component designed to assess speaking and writing.

- **Mid-Term Tests** with Answer Key
These should be given out after having completed U4.
- **Final Tests** with Answer Key
These should be given out after having completed U8.

The Big Question: How does music affect you?

- **Student's Book & Workbook**

Unit Opener

Visual prompts establish context and promote discussion

Vertical orientation of some sections to conform to visual requirements

Audios available on CD and in the Digital Book

Timed game-like activity

Vocabulary

Insight to language or content

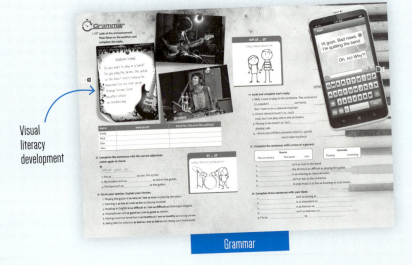

Visual literacy development

Grammar

Tips for skills development

Two skills per unit

Skills development tasks

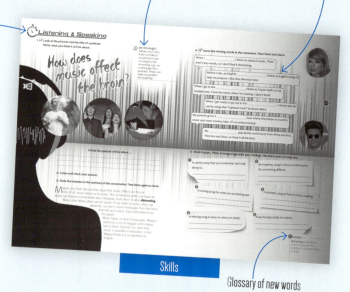

Skills

Glossary of new words

- **Student's Book & Workbook**

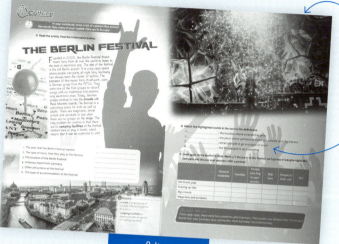

Content relevant to students' lives

Level-appropriate language encourages learner engagement

Culture

Sample of the project

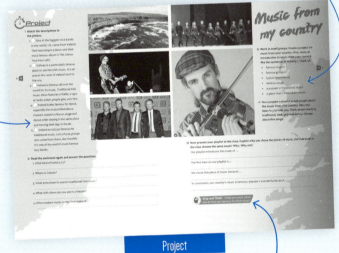

Linguistic and conceptual preparation for the project

Digital options for the project in the Teacher's Guide

Project

Critical thinking tasks

Activities for fast finishers

Just for Fun

Topics expand on the unit theme

Review

More practice with unit grammar and vocabulary

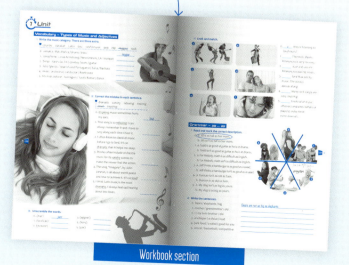

Workbook section

0 Why do we learn English?

Grammar	Vocabulary
Present Continuous (future meaning): Sasha and Nick <u>are having</u> a barbeque tonight. **First Conditional:** My parents <u>will</u> be angry <u>if</u> I lose my cell phone. **Past Simple and Past Continuous:** I forgot to turn on my alarm clock, so I didn't <u>wake up</u> on time for school. I took my umbrella to school because it <u>was raining</u>. **Might** and **Would**: One is that they <u>might</u> help people communicate with aliens. <u>Would</u> you like to see the Nazca Lines? **Should**: What <u>should</u> I do?	**Review:** aches and pains, habits, travel abroad

Listening
Identifying specific information

 **Teaching Tip**

Planning for the First Day of Class

When you are planning for your first day, here are some things to think about:

- Be flexible. The lesson, especially the first one, rarely goes exactly as you imagined it. Don't worry. Teaching is unpredictable.
- Don't try to control too much. Your goal for the first class should be to get everyone familiar with each other, learn each other's names and to introduce the course briefly.
- Let the students, and yourself, settle in. Often students are as nervous as you are and just want to get through the first day without any problems. Try to put them at ease by creating rapport and using humor.

 **Teaching Tip**

Letting Students Work Through Their Mistakes

Whether students are speaking, writing or reading English, allowing them to correct themselves will help them get a better grasp on the language. It may be tempting to interject with the correct pronunciation or spelling, but if a student can recognize his or her mistake and correct it, they are truly making progress.

Objectives

Students will be able to use the **present continuous**, **first conditional** and verbs in **past simple** to talk about **aches and pains**, **future plans**, **illnesses** and **conditions**.

Lesson 1   Student's Book p. 8

Warm-up

Students create and take a survey on their English-language learning to generate interest and activate prior knowledge.

- Write the following phrase on the board: *Studying English is important to me because / so that …*
- Students complete the sentence with their own ideas. Encourage students to come up with several sentences.
- Come together as a class and have students share their sentences. Write at least ten of them on the board.

Draw a scale similar to the following on the board:
0-Strongly disagree
2-Disagree
3-Slightly disagree
4-Partly agree
1-Agree
5-Strongly agree

- Have students rate their positions toward the statements, using the scale.
- Students form pairs or small groups and share their positions.

1 Look at the pictures and complete the sentences with the words in the box.
Students complete the sentences with the correct form of the phrases in the box to review present continuous with future meaning.

Answers
1. is playing basketball, 2. are going to the beach, 3. is seeing the vet, 4. are taking an exam, 5. am not doing anything

2 Unscramble the illnesses to complete the conversations.
Students unscramble the words to review aches and pains vocabulary as they complete the sentences.

Answers
1. fever, 2. bruise, 3. stomachache, 4. runny, 5. headache, 6. sore, 7. sunburn, 8. medicine

Stop and Think! Critical Thinking

How many reasons can you think of for learning English? Which is the most important to you?

- Remind students of the survey they took in the Warm-up.
- Students form pairs and brainstorm reasons to learn English.
- Come together as a class and have some pairs share their ideas.
- Then ask *Which is the most important to you? Why?*
- Students discuss with their partners.

Extension

Students should mingle to get to know each other.

- Prepare a list of questions and make copies. Here are some ideas (beyond *What's your name?* and *Where are you from?*):
  » *How long have you been studying English?*
  » *How do you spend your free time?*
  » *What was the last book you read?*
  » *What's your favorite movie?*
  » *Do you have any brothers / sisters / pets?*
  » *What kind of food do you like?*
  » *What other languages do you speak?*
  » *Do you play any sports?*
- Give one sheet to each student. Go over any vocabulary as necessary.
- Tell students they are at a party and they don't know each other. Explain that they need to ask questions to find out about each other. Explain that while the music is playing, they must speak with one student, asking and answering questions. They may make notes about their classmates' answers, but they should be talking when the music is playing.
- Play some music and encourage students to begin to mingle.
- After students have had a few minutes to talk with each other, turn the music off. When you have students' attention, tell them to find a new person to speak to and turn on the music again.
- Continue until students have had a chance to mingle, asking and answering questions.
- Come together as a class and have students share interesting facts they learned about each other.

Wrap-up

Students play a game of *Charades* to practice the vocabulary from Activity 1.

- Students form groups of three or four.
- They take turns acting out the phrases in Activity 1, without speaking, while other students try to guess.

▶ **(No homework today.)**

Unit 0

Lesson 2   Student's Book p. 9

Warm-up

Students play a game of *Hangman* to review vocabulary.

• Draw a hangman's gallows, like this, on the board:

• Choose one of the words from Activity 2, for example, *fever*, and write the same number of blanks as there are letters in the word on the board:

__ __ __ __ __

• Students form two or three teams. Team members take turns calling out letters. If a student calls out a letter that is part of the word, for example, *e*, write that letter in the appropriate blank or blanks. If it is not part of the word, draw the person on the gallows, beginning with the head. Draw one part of the body for each letter called that is not part of the word. Be sure to write the called-out letter to the side of the gallows so that students don't call it out again.

• The game is over when teams have either guessed the word, completed the word, or the body is complete.

• If time permits, have a student come up to the board and choose a word, while others call out letters and try to guess it. Award points for correct guesses.

3 Make the sentences true for you.

Students review the first conditional by completing the sentences with their own ideas.

Answers

Answers will vary.

4 Find 10 regular past simple verbs in the word search.

Students recall common past simple verbs as they do the word search.

Answers

```
S T O P P E D Q Z B S X
X G B K L W U G U G T M
X W B U A H S L E W U W
V J G Q N V W T Z Z D C
Q O P E N E D R P H I L
Q K L Q E V H I J W E O
S K A X D K K E J R D S
T R Y R W J Q D H E X E
A Z E B H Z Z H X I K D
Y M D H W O R R I E D Z
E C J D R O P P E D Q B
D W C B X D S M I L E D
```

5 Complete the table with the verbs from Activity 4.

Students categorize the past simple verbs they found in the word search according to how they are spelled.

Answers

+ed opened, stayed; *+d* smiled, closed, died; *Double the final consonant* stopped, planned, dropped; *y → ied* tried, worried

6 Think Fast! Can you think of an irregular past simple verb that begins with these letters: A, B, C, D, F, G, H, K, M, P, S, T, W?

Students do a two-minute timed challenge: they brainstorm irregular past simple verbs that begin with the letters listed.

Possible answers

ate, brought, came, did, forgot, got, had, knew, made, put, saw, thought, won

Wrap-up

Students have a race to practice the pronunciation of past simple endings.

• Write the following phonetic sounds, three times (one set for each team), horizontally at the top of the board: /d/, /t/, /id/.

• Elicit or provide examples of simple regular past tense verbs that have the endings, for example, *planned /d/, stopped /t/,* and *wanted /id/*.

• Students form three groups and line up in front of the board. Give the first person in each group a marker.

• Say a regular verb in present simple. Students race to write the verb in past simple under the correct column.

• Here are some verbs you can use: *open (opened, d), stay (stayed, d), smile (smiled, d), worry (worried, d), close (closed, d), try (tried, d); drop (dropped, t), help (helped, t), kiss (kissed, t), check (checked, t), laugh (laughed, t); shout (shouted, id), visit (visited, id), end (ended, id)*.

• When you have practiced the verbs you want to review, check each group's answers. The group with the most correct verbs wins.

➡ **(No homework today.)**

 Teaching Tip

Arranging Your Classroom

Here are a few things to keep in mind when you arrange your classroom:

• Change the arrangement based on your objectives. For pair work or group work, turn desks toward each other or in circles; for full-class instruction, consider a horseshoe shape.

• Don't change it too often. Let students develop some ownership of their classroom space.

• Maintain the same seating during assessment as you have when teaching the material. Students make associations between where they were when they learned something and when they're trying to recall it.

• Try having your desk it the back. This promotes a student-centered atmosphere.

Objectives

Students will be able to distinguish between the use of the **past simple** and the **past continuous** as well as the use the modals *would, might* and *should* to talk about **travel** and **habits**.

Lesson 3   Student's Book p. 10

Warm-up

Students play a game of *Catch* to review verbs.
- Bring in a soft ball or crumple up a piece of paper to use as a ball.
- Have students sit in a circle.
- Toss the ball to a student and say a verb, for example, *give*.
- The student makes a sentence using the verb. He then tosses the ball to another student and says a verb.
- That student makes a sentence.
- Continue until all students have had a chance to make a sentence.

7 Circle the correct options to complete the sentences.

Students determine whether the past simple or past continuous should be used in each sentence.

Answers

1. was looking, 2. had, 3. were shopping, 4. was surfing, 5. didn't wake up, 6. was raining

8 Listen and complete the conversation.

Students listen and complete the conversation with *would* or *might*.

Answers

1. Would, 2. might, 3. might, 4. might, 5. might, 6. would, 7. Would, 8. would, 9. might

Audio Script

Dom: I'm going to Peru with my parents.
Fran: Peru! Wow! Would you like to see the Nazca Lines?
Dom: The Nazca Lines? What are they?
Fran: They are giant drawings in the desert. You can't see them on the ground. You have to go up in a plane. Some experts think the Nazca Lines might be 2,000 years old.
Dom: Are they just lines in the desert?
Fran: No, the Nazca Lines are drawings of animals and plants. Look at this photo. What does it look like?
Dom: Hmm… yes, it might be an animal. I know! It's a monkey! So how many of these drawings are there?
Fran: About 70 designs, but they might find more in the future. Archaeologists work there all the time.
Dom: Why did ancient people make these pictures?
Fran: There are lots of theories. One is that they might help people communicate with aliens.
Dom: Aliens! No way! I would like to see the Nazca Lines with my own eyes.
Fran: Well, their purpose is a mystery. Would your parents like to see them, too?
Dom: I think they would. We will go and I might solve the mystery and become famous!
Fran: Good luck!

Extension

Students play a game of *Pictionary* to practice verbs.
- Write verbs on small pieces of paper, making as many sets as there are groups of four in your class.
- Students form groups of four and choose one person from their group to be the "drawer."
- Give the drawer for each group a card with the same verb.
- The drawer draws pictures to represent the verb. He / She is not allowed to speak or write words, only draw pictures.
- Once a group guesses the verb, the other groups stop. The group that guessed the verb is awarded a point.
- Groups choose another drawer to whom you give a new verb.
- Continue until you have practiced all the verbs you want . The group with the most points wins.

Wrap-up

Students play a game of *Tic-Tac-Toe* to review verb tenses.
- Students form two groups. Assign one group *O* and the other *X*.
- Draw a grid on the board with five squares horizontally and five vertically, similar to this:

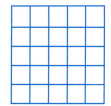

- Write a different verb, in various tenses, in each square, for example, *went, is finishing, had, was working, see*, etc.
- The *O* group picks a student to go first. He / She chooses a verb from the grid and makes a sentence.
- If the sentence is correct, the group places an *O* in the square.
- Play goes to the *X* team.
- Students play until one group gets five *X*s or *O*s in a horizontal, vertical or diagonal row. That group wins.
- Challenge your students by adding a question mark after the verb, meaning they have to make a question using the verb.

➡ **(No homework today.)**

Lesson 4 Student's Book p. 11

Warm-up
Students play a game called *Word-in-a-Word* to generate interest and activate prior knowledge.
- Write the word *VACATION* on the board.
- Students form pairs.
- Set a stopwatch for two minutes.
- Pairs write as many words as they can with the letters in *vacation*.
- When the stopwatch goes off, pairs come to the board and write their words.
- As a class, check the spelling of the words, crossing out any that are misspelled.
- The pair with the most correctly spelled words wins.

9 Complete the crossword puzzle.
Students complete the puzzle with travel vocabulary.

Answers

Across 1. passport, 6. stay, 7. train, 8. exchange, *Down* 2. suitcase, 3. resort, 4. flight, 5. guide

10 Circle the correct options to complete the blog.
Students practice using *should* and *shouldn't* as they complete the blog about study advice.

Answers

1. should, 2. shouldn't, 3. should, 4. shouldn't, 5. should, 6. shouldn't

11 Complete the sentences with the words in the box.
Students use the verbs in the box to complete sentences about habits vocabulary.

Answers

1. keep, 2. stream, 3. stay, 4. go, 5. work, 6. hang, 7. order, 8. sleep

Stop and Think! Value
How does having a balance between school, hobbies, friends and family affect your learning process?
- Draw a circle on the board and write the following words next to it: *school, hobbies, friends, family*.
- Ask *How much time do you think you spend on each?* Elicit some answers and begin shading in percentages, making a pie chart.
- Students draw a circle and complete their own pie chart according to how they spend their time.
- Students form pairs and compare their graphs.
- Then ask *How does having a balance between school, hobbies, friends and family affect your learning process?*
- Monitor as students discuss.

Extension
Students play a card game to practice *should* and *shouldn't*.
- Write scenarios on cards. Make as many sets as there are groups of three in your class.
- Here are some scenarios you can use:
  » *I want to speak English more fluently.*
  » *I want to be more popular.*
  » *I want a well-paying job.*
  » *I want to run a 10-km race.*
  » *I want to save [a certain amount of money].*
  » *I want to learn how to cook.*
  » *I want to be healthier.*
- Give each group a set of cards.
- Students deal out the cards equally to group members and turn them face-down.
- The first student turns over a card and reads it. The other students need to give them advice using *should* or *shouldn't*.
- Monitor, offering help as needed.
- Have students come together as a class and share some of the better, or funnier, pieces of advice.

Big Question
Students are given the opportunity to reflect on the Big Question.
- Ask students to turn to the unit opener on page 7 and think of why it's useful to learn English.
- Encourage discussion of the reasons and ask *Why do we learn English?*

⇒ **(No homework today.)**

1 How does music affect you?

Grammar	Vocabulary
Comparatives *as … as*: Emily's drums are <u>as big as</u> her. Emily's not <u>as tall as</u> Chris. **Gerunds:** <u>Playing</u> music is more fun than <u>listening</u> to music.	**Music:** classical, country, jazz, Latin, pop, rap, reggae, rock, world music **Adjectives to Describe Music:** catchy, dramatic, inspiring, loud, moving, relaxing, rhythmic

Listening	Speaking
Predicting meaning from pictures	Describing songs and feelings

How does music affect you?

In the first lesson, read the unit title aloud and have students look carefully at the unit cover. Encourage them to think about the message in the picture. At the end of the unit, students will discuss the big question: *How does music affect you?*

Teaching Tip
Using Music in the Classroom

There are many reasons to use music in your classroom. First, students can hear natural language in context. You can use songs to teach vocabulary and to practice target structures, since music improves concentration and memory. Here are a few tips for using music in your classroom:

- Ask students some questions about the title of the song you're going to play.
- Then listen to the song. Ask students to say how the song makes them feel.
- Listen to the song again. Focus on vocabulary, idioms and expressions in the song.
- Finish up with an activity. Here are some ideas: you can prepare a cloze activity with the song's lyrics or have students write another verse of lyrics.

Vocabulary

Objective

Students will be able to use **music** and **adjectives** vocabulary to describe music.

Lesson 1 — Student's Book p. 14

Warm-up

Students start thinking about the Big Question.
- Have some different types of music ready, for example, country, classical, Latin, jazz, world music, pop, rap, reggae and rock. Have students take out a piece of paper and pencil.
- Say *I'm going to play some music. I want you to draw or write whatever comes into your head.*
- Play the first piece of music. Let it play for about a minute. If you see students have finished writing, change the music.
- When you've finished playing all the music, have students form small groups of three or four. Have them share their drawings and what they wrote. Encourage students to express how the music made them feel.

1 🎧² **Listen and label the music categories for a new radio app.**

Students listen to musical selections and identify the type of music each is.

Answers

1. world music, 2. country, 3. reggae, 4. rap, 5. rock, 6. classical, 7. jazz, 8. Latin, 9. pop

2 Answer the following questions.

Students complete statements with music vocabulary so that they are true for them.

Answers

Answers will vary.

Stop and Think! Critical Thinking

Is it easier to play classical or rock music?
- Point out photos 5 and 6. Have students form pairs and think of at least three similarities and three differences of rock music and classical music. Accept any reasonable answers, for example, Similarities: *They both use many different instruments. They both are played to audiences.* Differences: *Classical musicians have to be able to read music. Rock musicians usually make more money than classical musicians. Usually rock music has lyrics, while classical music is instrumental.*
- Ask *Is it easier to play classical or rock music?* Have students discuss the question in pairs or small groups.

Extension

Students add to vocabulary and make an "audio" vocabulary notebook.
- Have students form pairs or groups of three and brainstorm other types of music they know. Students may come up with the following: *alternative, indie rock, punk, blues, R&B / soul, classical crossover.*
- Have students add the words to their vocabulary notebooks. Encourage students to include the following, when appropriate, with the entries:
  » a definition
  » an example sentence
  » an illustration
  » any synonyms or useful phrases
- Students can group this vocabulary set in any way that is logical to them. For example, Music you can dance to: reggae, country, pop, rock, reggae; Music that originated in the US: country, jazz, rap, rock; Music that uses guitars: country, jazz, world music, pop, reggae, rock.
- Have students individually find examples of each of the types of music. They can record their own voices along with the songs, as well as any useful information from their vocabulary notebooks. Students can do this in class if computers and appropriate software are available.
- Have students share their "audio" vocabulary notebooks with the class.

Wrap-up

Students consolidate music vocabulary with a game like Taboo, or Hot Seat.
- Write a type of music on the board and underline it, for example, <u>world music</u>. Then write words associated with the music under it, for example, *international, global, non-Western*.
- Place a chair in front of the class so that the board is behind it. Model by sitting in the chair. Explain that students should describe the underlined type of music to you without saying the music. The words, and all forms of the words, under the music word are "taboo," meaning students are not allowed to say them.
- Students form teams and choose a member to come up and sit in the "hot seat." Write another type of music and associated words on the board. Here are some examples:
  » country: western, guitar, the US
  » classical: violin, Mozart, Europe
  » Latin: Spanish, America, language
  » jazz: African American, New Orleans, trumpet
- Take turns having team members sit in the hot seat. Award points to the teams that guess the types of music.

▶ **Workbook p. 126, Activities 1 and 2**

Lesson 2   Student's Book p. 15

✔ **Homework Check!**

Workbook p. 126, Activities 1 and 2

Answers

1 Write the music category. There are three extra.
1. jazz, 2. country, 3. Latin, 4. classical, 5. pop

2 Correct the mistake in each sentence.
1. catchy, 2. relaxing, 3. dramatic, 4. inspiring, 5. moving

Warm-up

Students play a game of *Musical Chairs* to review vocabulary and generate interest.

- Set as many chairs as you have students, minus one, in a circle or oval. Make sure there's enough room between each chair so that students can sit down.
- Explain that you are going to play a song while students walk around the outside of the chairs. When the song stops, students should take a seat. One student will be left standing. The student left standing has to identify the type of music that was playing.
- Take away another chair and follow the same procedure, playing music while students walk.
- Continue as long as time permits or there is one chair / student left.

3 🎧³ **Listen to a band talking about music. Circle the correct answer.**

Students listen to the audio and choose the correct options to complete the sentences.

Answers

1. Orange, 2. weekend, 3. one song, 4. "Circle of Life," 5. reggae

Audio Script

SARAH: OK, people. We have a name for our group!
CHRIS: What is it, Sarah?
SARAH: Drum roll please, Zach. Orange Dream!
CHRIS: Orange Dream! I like it!
SARAH: And our first concert is next Saturday. We are playing in the school concert.
CHRIS: Oh! We are? How many songs are we playing?
SARAH: Just one, Chris. And we need to choose it now.
CHRIS: I have an idea—a country song. It's a moving tune. People cry when they hear it.
ZACH: Come on, Chris. It's a school concert. We need some catchy songs. Music that people can remember and sing along to.
SARAH: How about some jazz? I think it's really relaxing. I like listening to it in the morning when I have breakfast.
CHRIS: The concert is at night, Sarah, not breakfast time. Olivia? What's your idea?
OLIVIA: I think we should play a song from a musical. What about "Circle of Life" from *The Lion King*?
SARAH: Yes, Olivia! I love the music from *The Lion King*. It's so dramatic, so exciting!
ZACH: No way, guys. We're a rock band. We play loud music. Guitars! Drums! Noise!
OLIVIA: So what's your suggestion, Zach?
ZACH: I want to do a song that's inspiring. You know, a song that gives you hope and ideas. How about "Get Up, Stand Up" by Bob Marley?
SARAH: Yeah!
CHRIS: I like it!
OLIVIA: I don't know it, but… if everyone else is happy, I guess I am too.
ZACH: Great! It's a reggae song. I'll get my guitar and play it for you. It goes like this…

4 Complete the sentences with these words to describe music. Then listen again to check.

Students complete sentences with the adjectives to describe music used in the listening.

Answers

1. moving, 2. catchy, 3. relaxing, 4. dramatic, 5. loud, 6. inspiring

5 Think Fast! In your notebook, write an example of a song you play loud, a song that's moving, a catchy song and a relaxing song. Then write down the music category for each song.

Students do a two-minute timed challenge: they think of examples of music that fit the adjectives and identify the category of each.

Answers

Answers will vary.

Wrap-up

Students discuss when they listen to music to review the vocabulary.

- Elicit the words to describe music: *inspiring, loud, moving, relaxing, catchy, dramatic*. Be sure to include others that students know.
- Have students write down songs or bands that the words describe. Then tell them to think about when they listen to these songs or bands.
- Have students form pairs and discuss what kind of music they listen to and when.

➡ **Workbook pp. 126 and 127, Activities 3 and 4**

> 💭 **Teaching Tip**
> **Personalizing Activities in the Classroom**
> Personalizing activities has many benefits to students learning English. It allows them to communicate real information about themselves, which makes the material more meaningful to students. It also helps learners remember vocabulary and grammar more effectively. Personalization can be used at any stage of the lesson. Choose activities that get students talking about themselves, while practicing the target language.

Grammar

Objective
Students will be able to use **comparatives** and **gerunds** to talk about music.

Lesson 3   Student's Book p. 16

✔ Homework Check!
Workbook pp. 126 and 127, Activities 3 and 4

Answers
3 Unscramble the words.
1. classical, 2. country, 3. reggae, 4. rock, 5. rap
4 Look and match.
1. f, 2. d, 3. c, 4. a, 5. b

Warm-up

Students brainstorm instruments to prepare for the lesson.

- Elicit the types of music covered on page 15.

- Elicit what musical instruments students have come across in the unit or others that they know. They may produce the following: *the drums, the guitar, the bass, the piano, the violin*. Teach some others, for example, *the saxophone, the flute, the trumpet, the cello, the harp, the tambourine*.

- Have students form pairs. Ask them to make a graphic organizer in their notebooks to organize the instruments. They can make a chart or a mind map, for example. They can organize the instruments by types of music or by how you play them (pluck the strings, hit the top, blow through it).

- Have students share their graphic organizers with the class.

1 🎧⁴ **Look at the announcement. Then listen to the audition and complete the table.**

Students are exposed to the comparative with *as … as* as they complete the table with information from the audio.

Answers
Emily drums, yes, *Nick* guitar, yes, *Dan* guitar, no, *Alex* bass, yes

Audio Script

SARAH: Let's start the auditions! First one, please.
SARAH: What's your name?
EMILY: Emily.
SARAH: And you're playing the drums.
EMILY: That's right.
CHRIS: Emily's drums are as big as her!
SARAH: Shh, Chris! OK, Emily, play!
EMILY: What do you think?
CHRIS: Awesome but… You're a bit young for our band.
EMILY: What? I'm as old as you. I'm 15 too.
CHRIS: Really?
EMILY: Yes!
SARAH: Fine. You're in the band!
…
CHRIS: Oh wow!

NICK: Thanks, guys, my name's Nick.
SARAH: Nick, you're an amazing guitar player. You're in the band!
NICK: Cool! Er, my brother isn't as good as me on the guitar, but can he do an audition too?
SARAH: Sure.
NICK: His name's Dan.
CHRIS: OK, Dan.
DAN: Umm … Er …
CHRIS: Er, thanks.
SARAH: When did you start playing the guitar, Dan?
DAN: I started last week.
CHRIS: More practice needed, I think.
…
SARAH: Alex? Why are you doing an audition on the bass?
ALEX: Well, I'm not a great guitar player… and the bass isn't as difficult as the guitar. The guitar has six strings. The bass only has four.
SARAH: OK. Play something for us.
SARAH: That's nice, Alex. You're in the band!

2 Complete the sentences with the correct adjectives. Listen again to check.

Students practice completing sentences with adjectives from the listening to form the comparative with *as … as*.

- Direct students' attention to the ***as … as*** grammar box and read the example aloud.

Answers
1. old, 2. good, 3. difficult

3 Circle your opinion. Explain your choices.

Students choose the comparatives that complete the sentences according to their own opinions.

Answers
Answers will vary.

Wrap-up

Students practice *as … as* with a game.

- Write the following adjectives on the board: *busy, hungry, blind, quiet*. Make sure students understand the meaning of the adjectives. Act them out if necessary.

- Have students form pairs. Ask them to write phrases with *as … as* and the adjectives, for example, *as busy as*.

- Then write the following nouns on the board: *a beaver, a mole, a bear, a rabbit, a mouse*. Again, make sure students understand the meaning of the nouns. Draw pictures on the board if necessary.

- Students complete each phrase with an appropriate noun: *as busy as a beaver, as hungry as a bear, as blind as a mole, as quiet as a mouse*.

▶ **Workbook p. 127, Activities 1 and 2**

Lesson 4   Student's Book p. 17

> ✔ Homework Check!
> Workbook p. 127, p. 17
>
> **Answers**
> **1 Read and mark the correct description.**
> 1. a, 2. a, 3. b, 4. a, 5. b
> **2 Write the sentences.**
> 1. Mother isn't as old as Grandmother. 2. I am as old as my twin brother. 3. A whisper isn't as loud as a shout. 4. Junk food is not as good for you as a salad. 5. Soccer is as competitive as basketball.

Warm-up
Students review the spelling of vocabulary.
- Have students take out pieces of paper and cut them into cards. Each student should have a total of six cards.
- Divide the class in half by having students count off A and B. Have Students A write an adjective from the unit, for example, *catchy*, on each of their cards; Students B write music words from the unit, for example, *classical*, on theirs.
- Direct students to the vocabulary on pages 14 and 15 to check spelling.
- Students form pairs, one Student A and one Student B. They take turns saying a word on a card to each other. For example, Student A says to Student B, *catchy*. Student B then spells the word. If the student spells the word correctly, he gets the card. If not, Student A sets the card aside. Student B then asks Student A to spell *classical*.
- When students have finished trying to spell all the words, the student with the most cards is the winner.
- At the end of the activity, students should get their own cards back.

4 Look and complete Zoe's reply.
Students form comparatives using the structure *not as … as* and cues to respond to a text message.
- Point out the model sentence in the **not as … as** grammar box.

Answers
1. not as popular, 2. not as cool as, 3. not as fun as, 4. as good as

5 Complete the sentences with a noun or a gerund.
Students are exposed to gerunds as they complete comparative sentences.

Answers
1. The orchestra, 2. Playing, 3. Jazz, 4. The band, 5. Listening

6 Complete these sentences with your ideas.
Students personalize the comparative with *as … as* by completing sentences.

Answers
Answers will vary.

Wrap-up
Students practice *not as … as* with a game.
- Have students take out their cards from the Warm-up.
- Have students form A-B pairs again. They should lay their cards face down.
- Students take turns turning over an adjective card and a noun card. The other students should make a sentence using the noun, the adjective and *as … as*, for example, *Classical is not as catchy as reggae*.
- Accept any answers, even if they are a little silly, as long as they are grammatically correct.

 Workbook p. 128, Activities 3–5

> 🐝 **Teaching Tip**
> **Maximizing Oral Communication**
> Students need to be speaking English as much as possible. Getting students to speak in the target language in class is always challenging. Here are some tips to help:
> » Keep teacher talk to a minimum. Try using choral responses when first teaching a new structure. Do this in preparation for freer-speaking activities.
> » Consider students' individual needs. It is important to focus on each student and the skills that are most important for them. Try to tailor your instruction, at least some of the time, to each of your students.
> » Think of times when learning was enjoyable for you. Try to emulate those teaching styles.
> » Allow enough time. When you talk to a student, allow wait time for the response. When they struggle with a certain skill or structure, gently help them over this hurdle.

Listening & Speaking

Objective
Students will be able to predict what a listening text is about by reading its title and looking at some images.

Lesson 5   Student's Book p. 18

> ✔ **Homework Check!**
> Workbook p. 128, Activities 3–5
>
> **Answers**
> **3 Read and circle the correct gerund or noun.**
> 1. Rock, 2. Playing, 3. The orchestra, 4. The bass, 5. Ice skating
>
> **4 Read and underline the gerund or noun. Then match.**
> 1. <u>Singing</u> f, 2. <u>Playing</u> c, 3. <u>Reggae</u> d, 4. <u>Rock</u> a, 5. <u>Dancing</u> b
>
> **5 Read and fill in the blanks to express your opinion.**
> Answers will vary.

Warm-up
Students express their opinions to generate interest and prepare for the listening.
- Write the following statements on the board:
  - » Listening to music helps you study better.
  - » Listening to loud music is bad for you.
  - » Listening to music when you exercise helps you to relax.
  - » Listening to music can help you learn a language.
- Ask students if they agree or disagree with the statements.
- Students form small groups of three to discuss their opinions.

1 **Look at the pictures and the title of a podcast. Write what you think it will be about.**
Students examine the contextual material to predict what the listening will be about.

Answers
Answers will vary.

Audio Script
JOSH: I'm here with blogger Megan Hall.
MEGAN: Hi, Josh.
JOSH: Hello. So our question today is, how does music affect our brains? Megan?
MEGAN: Well, music helps people study. When we listen to music, we have to concentrate a little harder. When we concentrate, our brains work more.
JOSH: Uh-huh.
MEGAN: But listening to loud music isn't as good as listening to normal music. Loud music is very distracting.
JOSH: In what other situations can music help?
MEGAN: Sports.
JOSH: Sports? How?

MEGAN: When we exercise, we feel pain. The body tells the brain to stop and relax. When we listen to music at the same time, we don't notice these messages from the brain.
JOSH: So with music, we can exercise for longer?
MEGAN: Exactly.
JOSH: What is the best music to listen to when doing sports?
MEGAN: Fast music is best because it makes you move fast. For example, jazz isn't as good as rap when exercising.
JOSH: What other ways does listening to music affect the brain?
MEGAN: It also helps learning languages.
JOSH: How?
MEGAN: Singing new phrases helps people remember them. I tried this myself. I'm learning Spanish, so I listen to Latin music and I sing new sentences while I listen. I'm learning a lot.
JOSH: So music should be an important part of education.
MEGAN: Absolutely. For me, music is as important as math.
JOSH: Megan, thank you. It's been inspiring.

2 Listen and check your answer.
Students listen to the podcast and identify what it is about. Draw students attention to the **Be Strategic!** box and read it aloud.

3 Circle five mistakes in this summary of the conversation. Then listen again to check.
Students read the summary and identify five inaccuracies. They listen to the podcast again to verify their answers.

Answers
1. five ways (three ways), 2. concentrate less (concentrate more), 3. Jazz (Fast music), 4. reggae (Latin music), 5. English (math)

Wrap-up
Students discuss their reactions to the listening.
- Go around the room and ask a few students to restate one point from the listening, saying how music affects the brain. If necessary, write the following key words and phrases on the board: *study, loud music, exercise, language*. Elicit statements similar to the following: *Music helps people study. Loud music is distracting.*
- Ask students to say what new information they learned from the listening.

 Workbook p. 129, Activities 1 and 2

> **Teaching Tip**
> **Managing Fast Finishers**
> Some students complete activities more quickly than others, so it's a good idea to have a few extra activities on hand. Students can work on the *Just for Fun* pages individually and then check their answers in the back of the Student's Book. The *Just for Fun* activities for this unit are on page 26.

Lesson 6 — Student's Book p. 19

✔ **Homework Check!**

Workbook p. 129, Activities 1 and 2

Answers

1 Read the article and label each section.
1. Advertise, 2. Interview, 3. Practice, 4. Play live shows and record, 5. Market your band, 6. Most importantly, enjoy

2 Read the article again and circle T (True) or F (False).
1. F, 2. T, 3. T, 4. F

Warm-up

Students review adjectives with a race to prepare for the lesson.

- Have students count off to form teams of five or six.

- Tell students that you will say a noun. Students should write as many adjectives as they can think of to describe the noun until you say *Stop!* Then they pass the marker to the student behind them and go to the back of their team's line. Students cannot help the student who is writing and students cannot use an adjective more than once.

- Have teams line up in front of the board and give the first student a marker. Say a noun from the unit, for example, *classical music*. Give students five or ten seconds to write as many adjectives as they can. Then say *Stop!*

- Say another noun for the next student.

- When all students have had a chance to write adjectives, stop the game. Check for appropriateness of adjectives and proper spelling, eliciting corrections from students.

4 🎧⁶ Guess the missing words in the comments. Then listen and check.

Students complete the sentences with their best guesses. Then they listen to the audio and check their answers.

Answers

top to bottom study, test, gym, evening, dance, neighbors

Audio Script

SPEAKER 1: "When I study, I listen to classical music. There aren't any words, so I don't find it distracting."
SPEAKER 2: "Before I take an English test, I listen to English songs to help me prepare. I like One Direction best."
SPEAKER 3: "When I go to the gym, I listen to Taylor Swift on my headphones. I love her music when I'm running. I play it loud!"
SPEAKER 4: "When I get ready to go out in the evening, I always put on catchy songs like 'Uptown Funk' by Bruno Mars."
SPEAKER 5: "My parents go to a dance class where they listen to country music and wear cowboy hats. It's so embarrassing!"
SPEAKER 6: "My neighbors play all this world music from Africa and Asia. I like it, but I hear it all the time—through the walls. I want to complain, but my parents won't let me!"

5 Work in pairs. Think of songs to go with your feelings. Use these notes to help you.

In a speaking pairwork activity, students discuss which songs they think best fit different moods.

Answers

Answers will vary.

Wrap-up

Students do a mingle activity to review the lesson.

- Write the following phrase on the board: *Find someone who …* and elicit a few statements to complete related to music. Some statements may include *Find someone who listens to music when he or she studies. Find someone who likes Bruno Mars.*

- Have students create a "Find Someone Who" sheet, using the vocabulary and topics from the unit and their own ideas. Be sure each student creates his or her own sheet. Have them number the statements and draw lines next to them to write their classmates' names.

- Review the question form of the example statements: *Do you listen to music when you study? Do you like Bruno Mars?*

- When students have finished, have them stand up and ask each other questions. If you have music, you can play it in the background.

- The first student to complete his or her sheet is the winner.

➡ **Workbook p. 129, Activity 3**

Preparing for the Next Lesson

Ask students to watch an introduction to Berlin music festivals: https://goo.gl/sS7zcw or invite them to look around on the web site: http://goo.gl/e4Uvad.

 Culture

Objective
Students will be able to talk about a music festival.

Lesson 7   Student's Book p. 20

> ✔ Homework Check!
> Workbook p. 129, Activity 3
> Answers
> 3 Use the ideas below to write about a band you would like to start.
> Answers will vary.

▶ 22 **Warm-up**
Students say what they know about Berlin to generate interest.
- Write the word *Berlin* on the board. Ask students to share what they know about the city.
- Tell students they are going to read about a music festival in Berlin. Ask them to look at the phrases under the reading and predict the answers. Tell them that they will read to find out.

1 Think Fast! In your notebook, make a list of capital cities around the world. How many of your capital cities are in Europe?
Students do a three-minute timed challenge: they list as many capital cities of countries as they can think of. Then they count how many of the cities on their list are in Europe and compare results with a classmate.

2 Read the article. Find the information below.
Students read the article and then scan it to find the information to answer the questions.
   Answers
   1. 2005, 2. electronic pop, 3. the old Berlin airport,
   4. Kraftwerk, 5. magicians, street artists, acrobats,
   6. hotels

Extension
Students create their "dream" music festival.
- Ask students to think about the music and bands that they like.
- Have students form groups of three or four.
- Ask *What kind of information do you find on a music festival poster?* Elicit or provide the following:
   » Place (or venue)
   » Dates and times
   » Bands that will play there
   » Ticket cost
- Provide markers, magazines (to cut pictures out of), glue and any other materials that students can use. Alternatively, have them bring materials in.
- Have students work in their groups to make posters for their "dream" music festival.

Wrap-up
Students discuss their opinions on a festival.
- Have students form small groups of three or four to discuss the following questions:
   » Do you think you would like to go to the Berlin Festival? Why or why not?
   » Have you ever been to a music festival? Tell your group about it.
   » Are there some types of music that are better at music festivals? Explain.
- Come together as a class and have a few students share their opinions.

▶ **(No homework today.)**

 Teaching Tip
Using Project-based Learning in the Classroom
Group projects are a great way to put into practice skills that your students are learning in class. Whether they are small or large group projects, or an entire class project, they can be a welcome break from everyday lessons. Here are some tips:
- Whenever possible, provide a model of some kind. Either base your project around something students have been exposed to in the Student's Book or find a model to bring in to class.
- Give students clear guidelines to follow. Design a plan that lays out clear steps and gives students enough support.
- Provide enough time for students to complete the project, even if this means students take time to work on it outside of class.
- Make sure the project is meaningful to students. If they are interested in the topic and the project, they'll produce something worthwhile.

Lesson 8   Student's Book p. 21

Warm-up
Students retell the reading using key words and phrases.
- Elicit key words and phrases from the reading and write them on the board, or write the following key words and phrases on the board: *2005, electronic pop, airport, techno, Kraftwerk, 1970s, electric instruments, kids and adults, magicians, street artists, acrobats, hotels.*
- Students form pairs and take turns retelling the reading, using the prompts on the board and their own words.

3 Match the highlighted words in the text to the definitions.
Students determine the meaning of the highlighted words from context and match each with its definition.

Answers
1. site, 2. stage, 3. draws, 4. pioneers

4 Look again at the Berlin Festival. Mark (✓) the parts of the festival each group of people might like. Compare and discuss your answers with a partner.
In a personalization and speaking activity, students determine which aspects of the festival would appeal to different groups of people.
- Draw students' attention to the **Guess What!** box. Tell them that from 1949–1990, there were two countries called Germany. The country was divided after the Second World War. East Germany was communist. West Germany was a democracy.

Answers
Answers will vary.

Wrap-up
Students review material with a game.
- Draw a football field on your board like this:

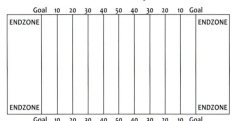

- Have students form two teams. Draw an X or another symbol at the end of each side of the field. If possible, use magnets that you can move easily up "the field." Flip a coin to see which team goes first.
- Have questions based on the lesson ready. Here are some examples:
  » What country is Berlin the capital of? (Germany)
  » When was the Berlin Festival founded? (2005)
  » Where is it held? (the old Berlin Airport)
  » Which band first played techno? (Kraftwerk)
  » What activities take place at the festival for kids? (magicians, street artists and acrobats)
  » Where do visitors have to stay when they come to the festival? (hotels)
  » What is a location where an event happens? (a site)
  » What is the place where performers stand in a concert? (the stage)
  » What is another way to say *attracts*? (draws)
  » What are the first people to do something called? (pioneers)
- Have team members take turns with "the ball," that is, answering questions. Depending on your students, you may allow other team members to help, or you may wish to make it more challenging by having students answer independently.
- If a team member answers the question correctly, move the X up the field one line and ask the team another question. If the team member misses the question, then it's the other team's turn.
- Continue as time permits and students are engaged.

Objectives
Students will be able to make a playlist of music from their country.

Lesson 9 — Student's Book pp. 22 and 23

Warm-up
Students use the KWL strategy to activate prior knowledge and generate interest.
- Tell students they are going to learn some things about Irish music.
- Write the following questions on the board:
  » What do I **K**now?
  » What do I **W**ant to know?
  » What did I **L**earn?
- Ask students to think about what they know about Irish music and what they want to know.
- Draw a chart similar to the following on the board:

Know	**W**ant to know	**L**earn

- Students form small groups of three or four to discuss what they know and want to know about Irish music.
- Students fill in the K and W columns of their charts.
- Come together as a class and have students share their thoughts. Write some of the things they know and want to know on the board.
- Have students set their charts aside to use at the end of the lesson.

1 Match the descriptions to the photos.
Students match descriptions of Irish music to the photos that correspond to each.

Answers
1. b, 2. a, 3. e, 4. d, 5. c

2 Read the sentences again and answer the questions.
Students answer comprehension questions based on the reading.

Answers
1. U2 is a rock band. 2. Galway is in the west of Ireland next to the sea. 3. The fiddle is used in traditional Irish music. 4. You can see a dance show in a theater. 5. Pop groups like *Westlife* come from Ireland.

3 Work in small groups. Create a project on music from your country. First, write an introduction to music from your country like the sentences in Activity 1.
Groups think about music in their own country and gather their thoughts in sentences, using Activity 1 as a model.

The Digital Touch
To incorporate digital media in the project, suggest one or more of the following:
- Students can create a playlist on http://www.listube.com.
- For a list of ways to create online video playlists, go to this site: http://goo.gl/kBQlsX.

Note that students should have the option to do a task on paper or digitally.

Wrap-up
Students use the KWL chart to review what they've learned.
- Draw students' attention to the KWL chart on the board. Have them take out their charts.
- Ask *What did you learn about Irish music?*
- Students complete the final column, L, of their charts.
- Have students meet in their groups and discuss the information in their charts and compare the information in their playlist introductions.

Teaching Tip
Using KWL Charts
KWL (Know, Want to know and Learn) is an effective strategy that combines before-reading, during-reading and after-reading activities. Here is a step-by-step guide for using KWL charts:
- Have students prepare a KWL chart, similar to the one in the Warm-up. Activate students' prior knowledge by having them generate, either individually or in groups, what they **know** about the topic or the text they will be reading.
- Then help students to generate a purpose for reading. Students think of questions about the topic they **want** or need to know. Guide students to look for answers to these questions as they read. Having these questions helps students monitor their own comprehension.
- When students have finished reading, they provide a record of what they have **learned**. Students write down information they have gained from the reading, some of which may answer the questions they wanted to know.

Lesson 10 Student's Book p. 23

Warm-up

Students activate prior vocabulary knowledge and generate interest with a game.
- Play a game called Make the Most Words to review vocabulary. Write one of the longer words or phrases from the unit on the board, for example, *instruments*, *traditional* or *world music*.
- Students work in pairs to make as many words as they can with the letters of the word on the board.
- Set a time limit of a few minutes. When the time is up, have pairs read out their words. If a word is read and another pair has it on their list, they should cross the word out.
- After all students have read out their words, the students with the most words left (spelled correctly, of course) win.

4 Now prepare a playlist to tell people about the music from your country. Use your ideas in 3 to help you. Think about classical, traditional, rock, pop and dance. Choose about five songs.
Students work on creating their playlist in their project groups.

5 Now present your playlist to the class. Explain why you chose the pieces of music. Did everyone in the class choose the same music? Why / Why not?
Groups present their projects and discuss each other's playlists as a class.

Stop and Think! Critical Thinking

What are some other places that are famous for their music?
- Elicit the types of music you have covered in the unit: *country, classical, Latin, jazz, world music, pop, rap, reggae, rock* and any others students know, and write them on the board.
- Ask pairs or small groups to brainstorm musicians or bands for each type of music.
- Come together as a class and have students share their ideas. Write some of the musicians and band names on the board under the corresponding types of music.
- Ask *Do you know where the musicians or bands are from?* See what students know and offer information you know.
- Then ask *What are some other places that are famous for their music?*
- Lead either a whole-class discussion or have students break into groups of four or five to discuss.

Wrap-up

Students create a bar graph to explain choices for their projects.
- Show students a bar graph similar to this one:

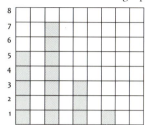

- Ask *What is the purpose of a bar graph?* Elicit or provide *to show and compare data*.
- Tell students that they will make a bar graph showing the types of music in the playlists.
- Have students form new groups, one student representing each group from the project.
- Tell students to follow these steps to make a bar graph:
  » Make a chart listing the types of music on one side and the number of students who chose that music on the other.
  » Decide on a title for your graph, for example, *Class Playlists*.
  » Draw and label the vertical and horizontal lines, or axes.
  » Write the names of the music types where the bars will be.
  » Label the vertical axis, for example, *Number of Students*.
  » Draw bars to show the total for each playlist.
- When they have finished, have students take turns explaining their bar graphs to the class.

▶ **Workbook p. 128, Activity 1 (Review)**

 *Review*

Objectives
Students will be able to use **comparatives** and adjectives to describe **music** vocabulary.

Lesson 11 Student's Book p. 24

✔ Homework Check!
Workbook p. 128, Activity 1
Answers
1 Write sentences using a word from each column.
Answers will vary.

Warm-up
Students list the vocabulary and grammar they have learned in the unit.
- Ask students to think of what they've learned in this unit.
- Elicit and list the vocabulary and grammar on the board. Vocabulary: types of music: *classical, country, jazz, Latin, pop, rap, reggae, rock, world music*; adjectives to describe music: *catchy, dramatic, inspiring, loud, moving, relaxing, rhythmic*. Grammar: comparatives with *as … as* and gerunds.

1 Order the letters to make music words.
Students unscramble the vocabulary words to complete the sentences.
Answers
1. country, 2. Latin, 3. world, 4. reggae, 5. jazz, 6. Pop, 7. rock

2 Match to make sentences. There's one extra.
Students match the types of music to their descriptions.
Answers
1. e, 2. b, 3. a, 4. f, 5. d, 6. c

3 Read the sentences and circle the correct emoticon.
Students identify whether each sentence corresponds to a happy or a sad emotion.
Answers
1. ☹, 2. ☺, 3. ☺, 4. ☹, 5. ☺, 6. ☹

Wrap-up
Students review the vocabulary with a game.
- Review vocabulary with a game of Twenty Questions. Have students count off by A and B. Team A sits in a group on one side of the classroom, and Team B sits on the other side. One member from each team goes to the board.
- Whisper a vocabulary item, for example *world music*, to the students at the board. The students sitting take turns asking their team leader a *yes / no* question to guess the vocabulary item. Students are only allowed to ask *yes / no* questions, and the team leaders are only allowed to answer *yes / no*. Students can ask a total of twenty questions.
- The first team to guess the word gets a point. Two new students come to the board for a new word.
- Continue until all vocabulary has been reviewed. The team with the most points at the end wins.

➡ **(No homework today.)**

 Teaching Tip
Using Substitution as a Communication Strategy
One way that students gain fluency is by substituting a known word for the word they can't remember. In this way, learners are able to get meaning across, even when they can't access specific vocabulary. Playing games such as Twenty Questions or Taboo help build this skill.

Lesson 12   Student's Book p. 25

Warm-up

Students play a game with comparatives with *as … as*.

- Students form pairs. Tell each student to take out two pieces of paper, and number each one 1–6. They will fill in one list with six nouns, of any kind they like. (For example, some nouns could be *chocolate*, *giraffe*, *blanket*, etc.) For the second list, they will form the beginnings of sentences with comparatives, using *as … as* and words from each of the sentences in Activity 3 on page 24. (For example, *1. music is as loud as… 2. This song is as inspiring as… 3. This music is as relaxing as…*, etc.)

- When pairs have finished making their lists, have them switch lists with the beginnings of sentences. Students will complete the beginnings of their partners' sentences with the nouns from their own list.

- Pairs share the results with each other and choose the funniest or silliest sentences to share with the class.

4 Unscramble the sentences.

Students review the comparative with *as … as* by unscrambling sentences.

Answers

1. I'm as tall as my older brother. 2. Jack isn't as intelligent as you. 3. Paris and New York are as rainy as London. 4. Payton isn't as old as us. 5. Football is as good as other sports. 6. A meter is as long as 100 centimeters.

5 Complete the interview with the adjectives below. Then listen and check.

Students complete comparative structures with the appropriate adjectives.

Answers

1. round, 2. loud, 3. tall, 4. long, 5. white, 6. good, 7. scared

6 Complete these common as … as expressions with the words below.

Students complete common expressions that use the target structure with the words provided.

Answers

1. easy, 2. red, 3. cold, 4. dry, 5. quick, 6. light

❓ Big Question

Students are given the opportunity to revisit the Big Question and reflect on it.

- Ask students to turn to the unit opener on page 13 and think about the question "How does music affect you?"
- Ask students to think about the discussions they've had on music, the readings they've read and the playlist they made.
- Students form small groups to discuss the following:
  » How important is music in your everyday life?
  » Do you think there's such a thing as "good" music and "bad" music? Explain.
  » How does music affect you?
- Monitor, offering help as needed, particularly with vocabulary.

⭐ Scorecard

Hand out (and/or project) a *Scorecard*. Have students fill in their *Scorecards* for this unit.

▶ **Study for the unit test.**

2 What have you done so far?

Grammar	Vocabulary
Present Perfect: I've been a fan of the Cincinnati Bengals my whole life. Have the Bengals ever won the Super Bowl? They've never won the Super Bowl. **For, How Long, Since:** How long have you been a fan? I've been a fan for five years. I've been a fan since 2011.	**Life Experiences:** camp overnight, change your look, design your own web page, learn to play a musical instrument, perform in a play, ride a horse, sail a boat, travel by plane

Reading	Writing
Identifying signpost words in writing	Using signpost words

What have you done so far?

In the first lesson, read the unit title aloud and have students look carefully at the unit cover. Encourage them to think about the message in the picture. At the end of the unit, students will discuss the big question: *What have you done so far?*

Teaching Tip
Praising Your Students

Try to call attention to the things your students are doing that meet expectations because:

- It enables you to restate and reinforce expectations for student behavior in a non-negative way. By praising on-task behavior, you enable students who may have misheard you the first time.

- It shows your students that you're aware of what's going on in the classroom. When they see and hear that you see and hear everything, they know that even their smallest actions matter.

- It shows that you care about your students' progress. Offering praise reinforces your concern for your students.

Objective
Students will be able to use **life experiences** vocabulary to talk about things they have done.

Lesson 1 — Student's Book p. 28

Warm-up
Students have a race to activate prior knowledge and generate interest.
- Write the letters A-C-T-I-V-I-T-I-E-S on the board vertically. Model by quickly writing a few activities that you have done beginning with the letters. You don't have to complete the acrostic, but provide some words. Here are some examples:
    » Act in a play
    » Climb a mountain
    » Tennis
    » Improve my English
    » Visit Rome
    » Invent something
    » Talk on Skype
    » Invent a game
    » Eat sushi
    » Sing karaoke
- Have students form teams of four or five. Write A-C-T-I-V-I-T-I-E-S on the board, one for each team. Explain that they should come up with activities that begin with each letter.
- Set a stopwatch for a few minutes.
- Teams come to the board and complete their acrostic with words associated with activities. The first team to finish, or the team with the most words when the stopwatch goes off, wins.

1 Label the pictures with the words in the box.
Students match life experiences vocabulary with photos illustrating them.

Answers

1. ride a horse, 2. camp overnight, 3. change your look, 4. sail a boat, 5. learn to play a musical instrument, 6. design your own web page, 7. travel by plane, 8. perform in a play

2 Complete the survey.
Students rate the difficulty of the activities according to their own opinions.

Answers

Answers will vary.

Extension
Students prepare a pictograph to summarize the survey.
- Remind students of the bar graph they made to explain their projects in Unit 1.
- Say *You will make a pictograph to summarize the survey. What do you think a pictograph is?* Elicit or explain that a pictograph is a representation of numbers on a graph, using pictures.
- Draw a pictograph similar to the following on the board:

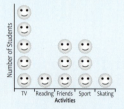

- Point out the labels on the horizontal and vertical lines. Ask students to tell you what the smiley faces stand for (number of students).
- Ask them to label the horizontal line with the activities in Activity 2.
- Students form teams and create their pictographs. Encourage them to use different symbols, perhaps representing each activity.

Wrap-up
Students discuss the results of the survey using the five *Wh-* questions.
- Elicit the following question words from your students: *Who? What? When? Where? How?*
- Draw students' attention to the survey in Activity 2. If necessary, elicit questions for the first activity: *When did you camp overnight? Who did you camp with? Where did you camp? How was the experience?*
- Students form pairs and use the question words to get information from each other about the survey. Encourage them to take notes on what they find out.
- Come together as a class and have some students share what they learned about their partners.

➡ **Workbook p. 130, Activity 1**

Lesson 2   Student's Book p. 29

> ✔ **Homework Check!**
> Workbook p. 130, Activity 1
> **Answers**
> **1 Categorize the words in the box in the correct activity.**
> 0. photos, 1. tent, cook stove,
> 2. identification, suitcase, 3. rehearsals, costume,
> 4. compass, life jacket, 5. sheet music, carrying case, 6. haircut, makeup, 7. saddle, reins

Warm-up

Students play a code-breaking game of *Mastermind* to review vocabulary.

- Write the same number of Xs as one of the verbs from the vocabulary phrases on the board, for example, *ride*. You may also include other activities your students have learned. For example, for the four-letter words *camp, ride, sail* or *play*, write *XXXX*.

- Go around the room, asking students to guess what the word is. Start a new line underneath the XXXX. If there are some letters that are contained in the word, but not in the same order, write a slash (/). For example, if the student says *sail*, write *X/XX*. If the letters are in the same order, put a checkmark (✓) in the corresponding position. For example, if the student says *hike*, write *X✓X✓*. If no letters are contained anywhere in your word, write *XXXX* again.

- Go around the room, having students guess words, and write the appropriate symbols until a student "breaks the code."

3 🎧⁷ **Listen. What activities in Activity 1 are the people doing?**
Students write vocabulary phrases identifying what the people in the listening are doing.

- Draw students' attention to the **Guess What!** box. Tell them that 18% of US adults have never flown in a plane.

Answers

1. sail a boat, 2. ride a horse, 3. perform in a play, 4. travel by plane, 5. design your own web page, 6. change your look, 7. learn to play a musical instrument, 8. camp overnight

Audio Script

1. Boy: Look at the sea! It's beautiful today!
   Girl: Dan! We're going too fast! Dan! Help!
2. Boy: Good boy. Good boy. I don't think he likes me.
   Woman: Come on! Get up on his back. That's right.
   Boy: It's very tall. I don't like this. I don't like animals.
3. Boy 1: To be or not to be. That is the question.
4. Woman pilot: Ladies and gentlemen, this is your captain speaking. I'd like to welcome you aboard this Delta Airlines flight to Chicago.
5. Girl: It's finished! It's online now! Come and look at it. Look. Click here. That's the home page. I did it all myself!
6. Dad: What have you done to your hair?
   Boy: I dyed it blue. Do you like it?
   Dad: No, I don't! You are not going to school looking like that!
7. Girl: I can't do it. It's impossible! It doesn't sound like a song! It sounds… awful.
   Mom: Don't give up! Let's look at it together. Right—play the first note.
8. Boy: Dad! Help! I can't do the tent! We're sleeping outdoors tonight.
   Dad: No, I'm not helping you. You do it. I know you can. I'll make the fire.
   Boy: Oh!

4 **Look at the pictures in Activity 1. In pairs, discuss which ones you have done.**
In a personalization activity, students discuss their own life experiences using the vocabulary.

5 **Discuss these questions.**
Students have a more in-depth discussion about their life experiences guided by the questions.

Wrap-up

Students play a guessing game.

- Ask students to think about the discussion from Activity 5. Ask them to think of one of their group members' answers and write it on a piece of paper. They should not write the student's name.

- Have students form new groups and take turns sharing what they wrote down. The other students try to guess which student said it.

➡ **Workbook p. 130, Activities 2 and 3**

Teaching Tip
Using Warm-ups
Your students need a chance to settle down and get their minds focused on the lesson ahead. Here are some things to keep in mind:

- Use warm-ups as "ice-breakers." These are essential for classes where students are new to each other or the teacher. They will allow everyone to relax and get to know each other.

- Students need to transition from speaking their own language to speaking English. Giving them some time at the beginning of class is a way to ease them into the tasks ahead.

- Warm-ups are not the time for identifying student mistakes. Warm-up sessions need to have the right flow for students to get ready for the lesson and to give them a chance to build up their confidence.

Grammar

Objective
Students will be able to use **present perfect** and *how long, for* and *since* to talk about their life experiences.

Lesson 3   Student's Book p. 30

✔ **Homework Check!**
Workbook p. 130, Activities 2 and 3

Answers
2 Match the underlined mistake to its correction.
1. e, 2. f, 3. h, 4. b, 5. c, 6. a, 7. g
3 Complete the sentences with the words in the box.
1. camp overnight, 2. perform in a play, 3. ride a horse, 4. travel by plane, 5. change your look, 6. sail a boat

Warm-up
Students review past tense forms with a game.
- Crumple up a piece of paper or bring in a soft ball.
- Model the game with a more proficient student. Say a verb in its base form, for example, *go*, and toss the ball to the student, asking him / her to say the past tense form, *went*.
- The student should toss the ball to another student and say a verb in its base form, and the game continues.

1 Read the text. Discuss what you learn about the categories below.
Students read and discuss personal facts about a teen.

2 Look at the sentences and answer the questions.
Students answer questions about the text they read for Activity 1.

Answers
1. … we won a competition. We appeared on the local news last month. I went camping with my cousin last year and we saw a grizzly. It was enormous! 2. Yes. 3. I've been a fan of the Cincinnati Bengals my whole life. They've never won the Super Bowl. I've never swum in the ocean. 4. a and b

3 Look again at Activity 1. Write the past participles of these verbs. Are they regular or irregular?
Students use the text in Activity 1 to help them remember the past participle of each verb and identify whether each is regular or irregular.

Answers
left to right, top to bottom been, irregular, swum, irregular, written, irregular, taught, irregular, seen, irregular, won, irregular

Extension
Students review past participles with a game.
- Draw a Bingo grid similar to this on the board:

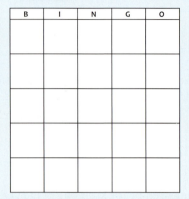

- Have students draw a similar grid on a piece of paper. Students should complete the grid by writing a verb from the unit in its base form in each box.
- Call out the past participles of verbs from the unit (*camped, changed, ridden*, etc.).
- Students should cross out the corresponding base forms as they hear them. The first student who gets five in a diagonal, vertical or horizontal row yells out *Bingo!*
- Continue playing until a few more students get Bingo. If time permits and students are engaged, you can play until a student has all squares marked off.

Wrap-up
Students review past participles with a game.
- Finish up the lesson with the same game you started it with, only this time, practice the past participle form as well.
- Toss the ball to the first student and say a verb, for example, *write*. The student should say *wrote*. Tell the student to toss the ball to another student, who says the past participle, *written*.

▶ **Workbook p. 131, Activities 1 and 2**

Lesson 4   Student's Book p. 31

✔ **Homework Check!**
Workbook p. 131, Activities 1 and 2
Answers
1 Read and circle the correct option.
1. since, 2. play, 3. has won, 4. went, 5. for, 6. have, 7. went
2 Look and complete the sentences with what the person has or hasn't done.
1. Steve hasn't performed in a play. 2. Sam and her family have camped overnight. 3. Marcela has played the guitar. 4. Robert hasn't ridden a horse.

Warm-up
Students play a game to review the present perfect.
- Working individually, students write two true and two false statements about things Josh has or hasn't done from the text in Activity 1.
- Students form pairs and read each other their statements. Students try to identify which of their partner's statements are true and which are false.

4 🎧⁸ **Listen to Josh and his friend Ashley talking about his favorite sports team. Complete the missing words.**
Students listen to the conversation and complete the sentences with the present perfect.

Answers
1. have, been, 2. Have, seen, have, 3. Have, met, haven't, 4. Have, won, haven't

Audio Script
ASHLEY: Wow, Josh, I've read your six facts. They're really interesting.
JOSH: Thanks, Ashley.
ASHLEY: How long have you been a fan of the Cincinnati Bengals?
JOSH: I've been a fan of the Bengals for years. All my life!
ASHLEY: Have you ever seen them play in the stadium?
JOSH: Yes, I have. Three times!
ASHLEY: Have you ever met any of the players?
JOSH: No, I haven't, but I hope I will one day.
ASHLEY: Have the Bengals ever won the Super Bowl?
JOSH: No, they haven't! But they have been close. They lost to the 49ers in 1989.
ASHLEY: I'm sure they'll win one day.

5 Complete the sentences with *for* or *since*.
Students determine whether *for* or *since* should be used in each sentence and complete the sentences.
- Draw students' attention to the **Guess What!** box and read the information aloud.

Answers
1. since, 2. for, 3. since, 4. since, 5. for

6 Use the prompts to ask questions to a partner.
Students use the cues to form questions in present perfect using *how long*. They take turns asking a partner their questions and answering their partner's questions.

Answers
1. How long has your family lived in your current home? 2. How long have you been a student at this school? 3. How long have you known your best friend? 4. How long have you sat at the same desk in this classroom? 5. How long has your English teacher taught your class?

7 Write three facts about you, your family or your life. Then share them with your partner and ask *how long* questions.
Using Activity 1 on page 30 as a model, students write three facts about themselves. Students tell their partner their facts and ask each other questions about their facts using *how long*.

Wrap-up
Students practice *for* and *since* with a game.
- Refer to the following key for the game:
  1. He's lived there _____ eight years. (for)
  2. I've worked at this job _____ I left school. (since)
  3. We've known each other _____ many years. (for)
  4. She's taught English _____ 2010. (since)
  5. I've been a fan of football _____ I saw my first game. (since)
  6. My grandparents have been married _____ almost 50 years. (for)
  7. I've been here _____ 9 a.m. (since)
  8. She's lived in Hong Kong _____ four years. (for)
  9. He's been in a bad mood _____ he got up. (since)
- Draw a Tic-Tac-Toe game on the board with numbers 1–9 in the squares.
- Students form two teams, one team X and the other team O.
- Ask the O team to choose a square by saying the number written in the square.
- Say the corresponding sentence from the key. The O team should decide whether to use *for* or *since*. If they are correct, they get an O in the square. If they are incorrect, the play goes to the X team.
- Continue until a team gets three Xs or Os in a row.

▶ Workbook p. 132, Activity 3

Teaching Tip
Teaching Listening Skills
Tell students a listening strategy is to read the exercise briefly and predict the missing information before they listen to the recording.

Reading & Writing

Objective
Students will be able to identify signpost words in writing and use signpost words.

Lesson 5 Student's Book pp. 32 and 33

✔ **Homework Check!**
Workbook p. 132, Activity 3
Answers
3 Complete the conversation with *for* or *since*.
1. since, 2. for, 3. since, 4. for

 Warm-up

Students review imperatives with a game.
- Play a game of *Simon Says*. Stand in front of the class and give instructions using the reporting phrase *Simon says* and imperatives. Use some phrases from the vocabulary, for example:
  » Simon says, "Stand up."
  » Simon says, "Lift your right arm."
  » Simon says, "Ride a horse."
  » "Play a musical instrument."
- If a student performs the action when you didn't say *Simon says*, he has to sit down. You can either explain this before the game or model it.
- Play the game until there is only one student left standing or as time permits.

1 Discuss these questions.
Students form pairs and discuss the questions about drawing.

2 Look at the sketches. Number the steps from 1–7.
Students are exposed to signpost words and phrases as they match the steps in the drawing instructions with the illustrations.
Answers
1. c, 2. g, 3. a, 4. e, 5. b, 6. f, 7. d

3 Circle seven signpost words or phrases in Activity 2.
Students identify the signpost words and phrases in the sketching instructions.
- Draw students' attention to the **Be Strategic!** box and read the information aloud.
Answers
a. Thirdly, b. Next, c. First of all, d. Finally, e. After that, f. Then, g. Secondly

Wrap-up
Students put signpost words and phrases in order and tell a story.
- Ask students to think of an activity they have done and know well. Here are some ideas: baking cookies or making a sandwich, rollerblading, playing a game, searching for something on the Internet.
- Students form pairs.
- Have pairs take out seven small pieces of paper. Students refer back to Activities 2 and 3 and write a signpost word on each.
- Pairs put the signpost words in order: *first of all, secondly, thirdly, then / next / after that, finally*.
- Students take turns explaining their activities to each other using signpost words and phrases.
- To extend the activity, have some students share their partner's activity with the class, explaining how to do it.

➡ **Workbook p. 133, Activities 1 and 2**

 Teaching Tip
Managing Fast Finishers
Some students complete activities more quickly than others, so it's a good idea to have a few extra activities on hand, otherwise these students may become bored and disruptive. One set of activities designed for fast finishers are the *Just for Fun* pages. Students can work on these individually and then check their answers in the back of the Student's Book. The *Just for Fun* activities for this unit are on page 40.

Lesson 6
Student's Book p. 33

> ✔ Homework Check!
> Workbook p. 133, Activities 1 and 2
>
> **Answers**
> **1 Complete the article with the correct headings.**
> 1. d, 2. c, 3. a
> **2 Correct the false information in the sentences.**
> 1. *Content* refers to the specific information you chose to include on your web page. 2. You can't have the same domain name as another web page. 3. You can follow these easy steps to design your own web page.

Warm-up
Students practice signpost words with a recipe.
- Write some food items on the board, for example, *strawberries, flour, yogurt, nuts, butter, peanut butter, sugar.*
- Students form pairs.
- Pairs come up with a recipe for using the food written on the board using signpost words. They can add ingredients, but they must use all the food items on the board.
- Have students share their recipes. Take a vote to see which recipe(s) are the best.

4 Cover the text. Look at the sketches only. Can you remember all the instructions? Read the text again to check.
Students look at the sketches in Activity 2 to see if they can remember the instruction for each step. Then they check their memory by reading the instructions again.

5 Work in pairs. Follow the steps to draw a cartoon of your partner. Is it easy or difficult?
Students form pairs to follow the instructions in Activity 2 and draw sketches of each other. Then pairs discuss whether it was easy or difficult to follow the steps and draw the cartoon.

6 In your notebook, use the pictures to explain how to set up a tent. Write the steps. Use signpost words.
Students use the signpost words they identified in Activity 3 to rewrite the instructions for setting up a tent.

Answers
1. First of all, choose a good location for your tent.
2. Secondly, clean the ground of sticks and stones.
3. Thirdly, put a tarp on the ground. 4. After that, / Next, / Then unroll the tent. 5. After that, / Next, / Then assemble the tent poles. 6. After that, / Next, / Then insert the poles into the material of the tent.
7. After that, / Next, / Then put the poles in the ground to raise the tent. 8. After that, / Next, / Then put pegs in the ground for the four corners of your tent. 9. Finally, connect the tent poles to the pegs. Your tent is now ready!

Wrap-up
Students tell a story to practice signpost words.
- Write a word or phrase on the board, for example, *sail a boat.* Ask students to write a word on a piece of paper and tell them not to show anyone. Encourage students to write a word related to the unit.
- Begin telling a story using the word or phrase on the board, for example, *Once, when I was sailing a boat, I came across a kitten floating in the water. First of all, I pulled down the sails and dropped the anchor to stop the boat.*
- Stop after a sentence or two and choose a student.
- The student continues the story, using her word and the appropriate signpost word, *secondly.*
- When that student has finished, tell students to try to guess which word that student has written on his / her paper and to write it down. Again, don't show it to anyone.
- The student who has just finished his part of the story then chooses another student to continue the story, using her word and an appropriate signpost word such as *next, after that, then.*
- Continue until all students have contributed. The last student must end the story using his / her word and *finally.*
- You may wish to have students do this in groups of five or six, depending on the size of your class.
- After the story is over, students share which words they guessed. The student who guesses the most words wins the game.

➡ **Workbook p. 133, Activity 3**

Preparing for the Next Lesson
Ask students to watch an introduction to Cappadocia: https://goo.gl/SzcFJI or invite them to look around on the web site: http://goo.gl/7DFLhA.

 Culture

Objective
Students will be able to learn and talk about activities people can do in Cappadocia.

Lesson 7   Student's Book pp. 34 and 35

> ✔ **Homework Check!**
> Workbook p. 133, Activity 3
> **Answers**
> 3 In your notebook, complete the outline below. Then write your plan to design your own web page.
> Answers will vary.

Warm-up
Students guess information to generate interest.
- *You are going to read about a special place in Turkey called Cappadocia. Let's see what you know.*
- Draw a square on the board. Then draw lines from one corner to the opposite corner twice to make four triangles.
- Have students take out a piece of paper and draw a similar diagram.
- Write four questions, one in each triangle, that relate to the reading, for example, *Where did people live in the past? Where do people stay now? What does the place look like? What can people do there?*
- Students form pairs and make guesses, filling in their diagram. Pairs compare their guesses.

Tell students they will read to find out the answers.

1 Think Fast! How many different methods of transportation can you think of? Have you traveled in any / all of these?
Students do a three-minute timed challenge: they think of examples of methods of transportation and say if they have traveled in them.

Answers
Answers will vary.

2 Read about Cappadocia in Turkey. Underline three activities that people can do there.
- Students read a text about a region of Turkey and identify three activities the text mentions people can do in the region.
- Draw student's attention to the **Guess What!** box. Tell them the capital of Turkey is Ankara. Istanbul was the last capital of the Ottoman Empire and nowadays is the largest city in Turkey.

Answers
1. cycling, 2. hiking, 3. hot-air ballooning

3 Complete the article on page 35 with questions a–i. There's one extra option.
Students read the Q&A article about hot-air ballooning and match the questions with their answers.

Answers
1. d, 2. h, 3. g, 4. a, 5. b, 6. f, 7. i, 8. e

Wrap-up
Students discuss the text with their diagrams.
- Have students take out their diagrams from the Warm-up.
- Students form new pairs (different from those in the Warm-up) and compare their answers.
- Students then correct their answers with information from the text.
- Ask students to say if any of the information surprised them and to share what they learned.

▶ **(No homework today.)**

 Teaching Tip

Brainstorming in the Classroom
Brainstorming is a useful tool to generate ideas about a topic or find solutions to a problem. Here are some tips that may aid brainstorming sessions:
- Foster dialogue. Encourage students to listen to others politely and respectfully as well as contribute.
- Generate answers. Frame the question that is the focus of the session carefully so that maximum ideas can be generated. Prepare a list of sub-questions that may help direct students if necessary.
- Set a time limit on discussion. The time set depends on the topic and students' interest. At the end of the session, be sure to have students summarize what was discussed.
- Don't overlook your part. Be sure to facilitate and manage the session without adding too much.

Lesson 8  Student's Book pp. 34 and 35

Warm-up
Students compare where they live with Cappadocia to prepare for the activity.
- Draw a simple table on the board with two columns. Write *similarities* over one column and *differences* over the other.
- Students form pairs and draw a similar table.
- Have students discuss things that are similar about Cappadocia and their area and things that are different.
- Pairs complete the table.
- Come together as a class and invite students to share their ideas.

4 Think about a place in your country or local area where people do an adventure activity like hot-air ballooning. Answer the questions in Activity 3 for your activity.

In a personalization activity, students think of an adventure activity people do in their country. Preferably, it should be an activity students have tried before. Students answer the questions in Activity 3.

5 Discuss these questions.

Students form small groups and discuss the questions about travel and adventure experiences. Encourage students to use present perfect in their discussions.

Stop and Think! Critical Thinking
What are the risks of hot-air ballooning?
- Direct students to the photo at the bottom of page 35.
- Say *Look back at the article on page 35. Why did the person say "It's quite frightening?"*
- Allow any reasonable answers, but they should include *Because the basket is not very large and the floor of it is very thin.* Students may also say that the balloon is very high off the ground.
- Ask *What are the risks of hot-air ballooning?*
- Students form pairs to discuss the question.
- Come together as a class and invite students to share their ideas.
- Ask those students who answered *yes* to the first question in Activity 5 if they would still go up in a hot-air balloon. If any students have ever gone up in a hot-air balloon, ask them to share their experiences with the class.

Extension
Students prepare a travel brochure.
- Ask students to think of what information is in a travel brochure. If possible, provide some examples either in print or online. Students may say the following: *Name of the place, things you can do there (activities, sports, etc.), what you can see there, places you can stay.*
- Elicit as much of this information as possible about Cappadocia: *Cappadocia, Turkey; ancient homes in rocks; go cycling, go hiking, go hot-air ballooning; extraordinary landscape, "fairy chimneys."*
- Provide paper or poster board, markers, paints and other art supplies.
- Students form small groups. They prepare travel brochures for Cappadocia or another place of interest.

Wrap-up
Students expand the activity with a guessing game.
- Write an exceptional ("once-in-a-lifetime") experience you've had on a piece of paper, for example, *go up a river in Vietnam on a bamboo raft*. Show this to students and read it aloud.
- Have students write down the answer that they gave for question 3 in Activity 5, their once-in-a-lifetime experience, on a small piece of paper. They should fold it up so that no one else can see it.
- Pass around a bag or a box for students to drop their papers in.
- Model the activity by "choosing" your paper and asking a few students *Have you ever gone up a river on a bamboo raft?*
- Have students choose a paper from the bag or box, making sure that it is not their own.
- Students mingle, asking about the activity they chose, until they match the student with the activity.
- When all students are matched, have students share their classmate's one-in-a-lifetime experience.

(No homework today.)

Objective
Students will be able to make a board game about life experiences.

Lesson 9 — Student's Book p. 36

Warm-up
Students predict the topic of a listening to generate interest and access prior knowledge.
- Draw students' attention to the icons and photo on page 36.
- Ask *What do you think the listening will be about?*
- Allow any reasonable answers and provide any necessary vocabulary. Pre-teach *shark, mouth-to-mouth (resuscitation)* and *first aid (kit)*.
- Write some student answers on the board.
- Tell students they will find out the answer in the listening.

1 **Listen and mark (✓) the activities Bailey has done.**
Students listen to an interview with a lifeguard and identify the icons for the activities the speaker says she has done.

Answers
icons 2 (gave mouth-to-mouth resuscitation) and 3 (applied cream to a jellyfish sting)

Audio Script
INTERVIEWER: Bailey, how long have you been a lifeguard?
BAILEY: Two months. This is my first job.
INTERVIEWER: Have you ever seen a shark?
BAILEY: No, I haven't. I've never seen a shark in my life!
INTERVIEWER: Have you ever saved someone's life?
BAILEY: Yes, I have. It was my first day at work. I saw an old lady in the sea. She disappeared under the water. I jumped in the water and I swam with her to the beach. I gave her mouth-to-mouth and I saved her life.
INTERVIEWER: Amazing! On your first day at work! Have you ever helped a person stung by jellyfish?
BAILEY: Yes, I have. A child was stung on the leg and I applied cream on it. I always have cream in my first-aid kit.
INTERVIEWER: This has been a very exciting first job for you!

2 Work in pairs. Check your answers in Activity 1.
Students form pairs and discuss their answers to Activity 1 using present perfect in their questions and answers, following the model.

3 In groups, think of three things that you have done in your life that the other students have never done. Write *have you ever* questions for each one.
In small groups, students brainstorm life experiences.
- Forming questions in present perfect, students determine whether they have come up with three things they have done but their group members have not.
- Groups write their questions in present perfect for each member's three unique experiences.

Extension
Students write about an experience.
- Have students write a descriptive essay about an exceptional experience.
- Prompt students to use the *Wh* question strategy for prewriting in class.
- Elicit question words: *Who? What? Where? When? Why? How?*
- Students form questions about their experience using the question words.
- Students spend time thinking about the answers to the questions. This is the information they will use for their essay.
- After students have finished the prewriting task, have them write their essays at home. Tell them to divide their essay in three parts. First they write an introduction to provide a context for their exceptional experience. Then they write the body of the essay where they answer the question words providing details. Finally, they write a conclusion where they explain why this exceptional experience was so special.
- If possible, give students some time to read each other's essays and give some peer feedback in class.

Wrap-up
Students practice the present perfect with a game.
- Play a game called *Two Truths and a Lie*.
- Think of three statements about yourself and things you have or haven't ever done, using the present perfect. Two are true and one is a lie.
- After you say these statements to your students, ask them to guess which statement is a lie.
- Students think of three statements about things they have or haven't ever done.
- Students form small groups of three or four and try to guess.
- To extend the activity, have students form new groups and try to guess. The student who guesses the most lies correctly is the winner.

Lesson 10 Student's Book pp. 36 and 37

Warm-up
Students peer-edit each other's work to prepare for the project.
- Have students take out the questions they wrote for Activity 3.
- Students form pairs and compare their sentences. Encourage them to edit and make changes as necessary. Ask them to focus on grammar, spelling and punctuation.

4 Complete the board game with the questions in Activity 3. Add more *have you ever* questions.
In their project groups, students add the questions they wrote for Activity 3 to the board game on page 37. Students write more questions to fill in all of the blanks on the board game.

5 Use the board game as a draft and follow the steps.
Students copy the board game on page 37 onto in a bigger piece of cardboard paper. Ask them to decorate their questions and exchange board games.

6 Play the game in pairs. Find a counter to represent you. Toss a coin to move. Heads = 1 square. Tails = 2 squares. Discuss the question in the square.
Students form pairs and play their board games following the instructions.

> **The Digital Touch**
> To incorporate digital media in the project, suggest one or more of the following:
> - Try this online tool for creating infographics: http://www.infogr.am.
> - Make your infographic and invitation using free software like Google Docs or Slides.
>
> Note that students should have the option to do a task on paper or digitally.

Wrap-up
Students review the present perfect and *ever* with a game.
- Write the starter question *Have you ever…?* on the board.
- Elicit a few phrases to complete the question, for example, *been to [Berlin], eaten sushi, owned a pet.*
- Tell students that they are going to make a *Find-Someone-Who* sheet. Tell them to write *Find Someone Who* on the top of a piece of paper.
- Students write eight to ten verb phrases that can complete the starter question *Have you ever…?* Next to each phrase, they should draw a line.
- When students have finished, have them stand up and mingle, asking and answering questions. Once they find a student who has done the activity they asked, they write that student's name and move on to the next question.
- Students continue to ask questions until they have asked them all. The student who has found the most people first wins.

 Workbook p. 132, Activity 1 (Review)

> 🍃 **Teaching Tip**
> **Encouraging Students to Take Responsibility for Their Learning**
> Empowering students to see themselves as the ones in control of their learning is one of the best things any teacher can give. Communicate with your students that they can be, and should be, proactive in their learning. The outcome will be students who know how they learn and study best, and who know how to take advantage of resources and methods. Here a few tips to get students to be in charge of what they learn:
> - If you assign a writing assignment, when possible, give students a choice of medium—a traditional essay, a film, a comic-book-style summary, etc.
> - Engage students in self-evaluation. You can do this in a more structured way, for example, with a survey mid- and end of year. You may also approach it in a less structured way by taking five minutes at the end of class to respond to the following questions:
>   » What did I learn today?
>   » What do I still have questions about?
>   » Could I use what I've learned to take a test, complete an assignment or accomplish something in my life?
> - The fastest way to empower students is to make their work matter in the real world, so get to know what is important to them.

Objective
Students will be able to use the **present perfect** and *how long*, *for* and *since* to talk about **life experiences** vocabulary.

Lesson 11 Student's Book p. 38

> ✔ **Homework Check!**
> Workbook p. 132, Activity 1 (Review)
> **Answers**
> **1 Make sentences about your experiences with the words in the box.**
> Answers will vary.

Warm-up
Students play a game to review vocabulary.
- Draw a hangman's noose on the board, similar to this:

- Choose one of the vocabulary items, for example, *ride a horse*. Put as many blanks as there are letters and set slashes between words: __ __ __ __ / __ / __ __ __ __ __.
- Students form three or four teams. Each team calls out a letter. If the letter is in the phrase, fill it in. If it is not, write that letter to the side of the noose and begin to draw the man on the noose starting with his head.
- Play until one of the team says the word or phrase or the man is "hung," that is, completely drawn on the noose.
- Continue with the rest of the vocabulary items.

1 Find six activities in the word snake. Then match them to the correct pictures.
Students identify vocabulary phrases and match them to the correct pictures.
Answers
1. change my look, 2. sail a boat, 3. ride a horse, 4. camp overnight, 5. travel by plane, 6. play the drums

2 Replace the words in bold with these words.
Students identify which words and phrases can be substituted for the words in bold so that the sentences still make sense.
Answers
1. for a week, 2. an opera, 3. a magazine, 4. her bike, 5. the bass, 6. paddle the canoe, 7. her hair, 8. in a helicopter

3 🎧¹⁰ Listen to five conversations. Write the number of each conversation.
Students match the conversations they hear with the experience each is about.
Answers
a. 3, b. 1, c. 4, d. 5, e. 2

Audio Script
1. A: Ow!
   B: What's that?
   A: That's my foot!
   B: Sorry! There's no room in this tent!
   A: Do you hear that?
   B: What?
   A: Rain!
   B: Oh no! This is the worst camping trip ever!
2. C: Here comes the king!
   D: Umm… what's my line?
   C: "Welcome, your majesty!"
   D: Welcome, your majesty! How is your daughter, the princess?
   E: Er… My SON the PRINCE is very well, thank you.
   D: son… prince… not princess. Oh no!
3. F: Look! Look! A dolphin!
   G: Wow! It's swimming very near us.
   F: Move closer! I want to take a photo.
   G: OK. Let me turn the boat…
   F: Now!
   G: Oh no! My camera!
   F: And the dolphin's gone, too!
4. H: What are you doing, Bill?
   I: I'm shaving my head.
   H: What? You'll have no hair left!
   I: It's OK. It's cool.
   H: Mom is going to be mad. You can't go to school like that.
   I: Really? I didn't know that. I've started now. I can't go to school with half my hair!
5. J: What's that noise?
   K: I don't know. I'm sure it's nothing.
   J: Perhaps we should tell the pilot.
   K: The pilot? What are you talking about?
   J: That noise! Perhaps something's wrong!
   K: Relax. It's all fine. Look! There's New York City below.
   J: I don't want to look out the window.
   J: There's that noise again!
   K: This is going to be a long flight.

Wrap-up
Students review vocabulary of the unit with a game of Charades.
- Model the game by acting out one of the actions, for example, put up a tent. Hold up four fingers to show that the phrase is four words. Then hold up four fingers again to show you are describing the fourth word, *tent*.
- Have students form groups of four or five and take turns to play.

➡ **(No homework today.)**

Lesson 12 Student's Book p. 39

Warm-up
Students review past tense and past participles with a game.
- Set a large container or trash basket in the middle of the room. Crumple up a piece of paper to make a "basketball," or use a soft ball.
- Students form two teams. Tell students they are going to play "basketball" and should choose names for their teams.
- Flip a coin, asking students to call "heads" or "tails," to see which team goes first.
- Say the base form of verb, for example, *ride*. The first student in the team who won the toss must say the simple past form and the past participle of the verb: *rode, ridden*.
- If the student gets the forms correct, he / she gets a chance to toss the ball into the basket. If he / she gets it in the basket, her team gets a point. If not, the ball goes to the other team who gets a shot.
- Then say the base form of another verb for the second team, and follow the same procedure.

4 Underline the correct option to complete the conversation.
Students identify the correct forms in the present perfect to complete the sentences.

Answers
1. Have you ever driven, 2. Have you won, 3. I've won, 4. I won, 5. Have you had, 6. I had, 7. I crashed, 8. Did you go to the hospital, 9. I've never been, 10. I broke, 11. I spent, 12. I've never broken

5 Complete the sentences using the Present Perfect.
Students form the present perfect using cues to complete the sentences.

Answers
1. 've / have never been, 2. has met, 3. has moved, 4. hasn't / has not rained, 5. 've / have learned, 6. has disappeared, 7. has lost, 8. hasn't / has not come

6 Complete the e-mail with *for* or *since*.
Students identify whether *for* or *since* should be used and complete the sentences.

Answers
1. for, 2. since, 3. since, 4. for, 5. for, 6. since, 7. since, 8. for

Extension
Students play a game of Jeopardy as part of the review.
- Play a game of Jeopardy in teams of four or five to review the language in the unit.

- Draw the following chart on the board, or you may wish to put it on some kind of presentation software:

Activity Verbs	Signpost Words & Phrases	Past Participles	Cappadocia
100	100	100	100
200	200	200	200
300	300	300	300
400	400	400	400

- Teams take turns choosing an amount and a category, for example, *Activity Verbs for 100*. You then ask them a question and if they answer correctly, that team gets a point.
- Play until all questions have been asked and answered correctly. The team with the most points wins.
- Here are some questions you can ask:

Activity Verbs
100: ____ a horse (ride)
200: ____ a boat (sail)
300: ____ overnight (camp)
400: ____ in a play (perform)
Signpost Words & Phrases
100: the phrase you use first (First of all)
200: the phrase you use last (Finally)
300: a phrase that means *next* (After that)
400: the word you use for the number two step (Secondly)
Past Participles
100: change (changed)
200: sail (sailed)
300: ride (ridden)
400: write (written)
Cappadocia:
100: What country is Cappadocia in? (Turkey)
200: What's the best way to see Cappadocia? (by hot-air balloon)
300: What is special about Cappadocia? (the extraordinary landscape)
400: What are *fairy chimneys*? (tall towers of stone)

Big Question
Students are given the opportunity to revisit the Big Question and reflect on it.
- Ask students to turn to the unit opener on page 27 and think about the question "What have you done so far?"
- Ask students to think about the discussions they've had about their past, present and future activities, the readings they've read and the board game they made.
- Students form small groups to discuss the following:
  » What's the most dangerous thing you've ever done? The most interesting? The most valuable?
  » Think about the goals you have for your future. How do you plan to accomplish them?

Scorecard
Hand out (and/or project) a *Scorecard*. Have students fill in their *Scorecards* for this unit.

 Study for the unit test.

3 How do you help at home?

Grammar	Vocabulary
Past Perfect (+,-): You <u>hadn't taught</u> her the rules. She destroyed the bed because she <u>hadn't gone</u> outside.	**The Household:** cupboard, drawer, garbage, laundry, living room, tablecloth, trash, yard **Phrasal Verbs:** clean out, hang up, pick up, put away, take out, throw away, wash up, wipe off

Listening	Speaking
Identifying key words	Convincing others

In the first lesson, read the unit title aloud and have students look carefully at the unit cover. Encourage them to think about the message in the picture. At the end of the unit, students will discuss the big question: *How do you help at home?*

Teaching Tip

Increasing Student Participation

Getting students to participate can be a challenge. Try the following suggestions.

- Try to arrange your room in a way that encourages active engagement. Consider moving the chairs to ensure students can see and speak with one another.
- Make it clear that all students should participate.
- Encourage students to ask questions throughout the lesson, not just at the end.
- Give students time to respond. Count to eight or ten after asking a question to make sure you're giving students enough time.

# Vocabulary

Objective
Students will be able to use **phrasal verbs** to talk about household chores.

Lesson 1 Student's Book pp. 42 and 43

Warm-up

Students identify items in a picture to generate interest and activate prior learning.
- Draw students' attention to the picture on page 41.
- Ask, *How many items in the picture can you name?*
- Students form pairs.
- Set a stopwatch for one minute.
- Pairs race against the clock to write down as many items as they can.
- When the stopwatch goes off, the pair with the most correctly spelled items wins.
- Students may identify the following: *a vacuum cleaner, a rake, a laptop, a cell phone, a hammer, fruit, vegetables, a frying pan, a list, a man, a woman, shopping bags, a dog.*

1 **Listen and circle the correct option.**
Students listen to the audio about the chores Mr. Stickman does and choose the correct preposition for each one.

Answers

1. out, 2. up, 3. up, 4. away, 5. up, 6. away, 7. off, 8. out

---

Audio Script

These are the chores Mr. Stickman did last week.
1. Mr. Stickman took out the garbage.
2. Mr. Stickman picked up his clothes from the floor.
3. Mr. Stickman hung up his clothes in the closet.
4. Mr. Stickman threw away the banana peel in the trash can.
5. Mr. Stickman washed up the dishes.
6. Mr. Stickman put away the bone in the drawer.
7. Mr. Stickman wiped off the table.
8. Mr. Stickman cleaned out the closet.

---

2 Look at Activity 1 and write the phrasal verbs next to their definitions.
- Draw students' attention to the **Phrasal Verbs** box on page 42 and explain how they are formed.
- Students identify the definitions of the phrasal verbs from Activity 1.
- Draw students' attention to the **Guess What!** box on page 43. Tell them *wash up* is used in British English. In American English we say *do the dishes.*

Answers

1. throw away, 2. clean out, 3. put away, 4. wipe off, 5. hang up, 6. pick up, 7. take out, 8. wash up

Extension

Students practice phrasal verbs with a treasure hunt.
- Write the two parts of each phrasal verb on separate cards or small pieces of paper.
- Stick them around the room.
- Ask students to race to find the parts of the phrasal verbs.
- If a student finds one part and another student finds the other, they should negotiate, for example, swap cards to complete the phrasal verbs.
- When all phrasal verbs have been matched up, the student with the most wins.

Stop and Think! Critical Thinking

Who does most of the household chores in your country: men or women, adults or children? Does everyone share the work equally?
- Read the **Stop and Think!** box aloud.
- Ask students to list the chores they do every week. They should write the chore, how often they do it and how long it takes them.
- Ask *How are chores divided up in your house?* Elicit a few answers.
- Then ask *Who does most of the household chores in your country? Is it women, men or children? How is it divided up?*
- Students form small groups of three or four to discuss.
- As a class have a few students share their thoughts.

Wrap-up

Students practice phrasal verbs with a Pictionary game.
- Students form groups of three or four.
- Set a stopwatch for two minutes.
- Students take turns drawing the phrasal verbs from the lesson while the other students try to guess.
- The group that has successfully drawn and guessed the most phrasal verbs when the stopwatch has gone off wins.

➡ **Workbook p. 134, Activities 1 and 2**

Lesson 2
Student's Book pp. 42 and 43

> ✔ **Homework Check!**
> Workbook p. 134, Activities 1 and 2
> **Answers**
> **1 Write the words in the correct column.**
> *pick up* these shoes, *throw away* the old newspaper, *put away* the dishes, the groceries, *clean out* the cabinet, *hang up* your coat, your shirts, the mirror, the laundry
> **2 Correct the phrasal verb.**
> 1. clean out, 2. put away / hang up, 3. throw away, 4. pick up / hang up, 5. take out

Warm-up
Students review vocabulary with a game of *Simon Says*.
- Model the activity by saying a command with one of the phrasal verbs and the phrase *Simon says*: *Simon says, hang up your coat*.
- Students act out the command.
- Then say a command without the phrase: *Put away your socks*.
- As students act out the command, explain that you did not say *Simon says*, therefore, they should not act it out. You must say *Simon says*, or the students who act out the command sit down and are out of the game.
- The last student or students standing win the game.

3 Cross out the words that don't work in each case.
Students identify which option in each sentence is not used with the phrasal verb.

Answers
1. the car, 2. garden, 3. door, 4. sneakers, 5. chair, 6. the cat, 7. laundry, 8. smartphone

> ### Extension
> Students review vocabulary with a board game.
> - Bring in one die for every four students. Make a board game similar to this one http://goo.gl/Aj5rTK with the household chores of the lesson.
> - Students get a counter (a pen cap, an eraser, etc.) and form groups of four.
> - Give each group a copy of the board game.
> - Students take turns rolling the die and moving that many spaces on the board. They follow the board's instructions.
> - The student who reaches the end first wins.

Wrap-up
Students race to write original sentences with phrasal verbs.
- Students form teams of four or five and stand in line in front of the board. Give each team a marker.
- Say a phrasal verb from the lesson, for example, *put away*.
- The first student in each line begins to write the first word of the sentence. He / She can only write one word and then passes the marker to the next student, who writes the next word. He / She passes the marker to the next student in line and that student writes another word.
- When the first team is finished writing a sentence, say *Stop!*
- Read each sentence, asking the class to determine if it's correct. If it's correct, that team gets a point. If it's not correct, the team to the right can earn a point by correcting it.
- Continue with the same procedure, calling out another phrasal verb.
- Continue as long as time permits and students are engaged. The team with the most points wins.

➡ **Workbook p. 134 and 135, Activities 3 and 4**

Grammar

Objective
Students will be able to use the **past perfect** to talk about household and pet responsibilities.

Lesson 3   Student's Book p. 44

> ✔ **Homework Check!**
> Workbook pp. 134 and 135, Activities 3 and 4
> **Answers**
> **3 Label the pictures with the correct phrasal verb.**
> 1. take out, 2. hang up, 3. put away, 4. pick up,
> 5. clean out / wipe off
> **4 Match the sentence halves.**
> 1. f, 2. a, 3. d, 4. e, 5. c

▶ 46

Warm-up

Students discuss their opinions on pets to generate interest and activate prior knowledge.
- Write the following questions on the board:
  » *Do you have a pet?*
  » *What are the advantages and disadvantages of keeping a pet?*
  » *What can you learn from having a pet?*
- Students form small groups and discuss.
- Monitor, offering help as needed.
- Come together as a class and have some students share their ideas.

1 When you have a pet dog, what responsibilities do you have? Make a list.
Students list things that have to be done to take care of a pet dog.
Answers
Answers will vary.

2 Read Jesse's e-mail and number the pictures 1–3 in the order they are mentioned.
Students identify the order in which things the dog did are mentioned in the e-mail.
Answers
top to bottom 2, 3, 1

3 In pairs, discuss the questions. Then read WonderVet's reply to compare your answers. Why do you think the dog behaves badly? Can you think of a solution?
Students discuss reasons for the behavior of Miss Woofwoof described in Activity 2. Then they read the vet's reply and compare their answers and solutions with those suggested in the reply.
Answers
Answers will vary.

Wrap-up

Students discuss their reactions to a text.
- Draw students' attention to the e-mail and the reply in Activities 2 and 3.
- Ask *Do you think WonderVet gives good advice? Why or why not? Have you ever had any of these problems with a pet dog? What did you do?*
- Students form small groups and discuss.
- Monitor, offering help as needed.
- Come together as a class and have some students share their experiences.

➡ **Workbook pp. 135 and 136, Activities 1 and 2**

🐝 Teaching Tip
Keeping Discussions Going
We use discussions often in our classrooms, sometimes to activate prior knowledge, sometimes to consolidate learning and sometimes to generate interest and personalize a topic. But what to do when the discussion isn't going so well? Here are a few tips to get and keep discussions on track:
- Make sure the point is clear. If students don't know what they're supposed to be discussing, there won't be much production.
- Keep things balanced. Try to avoid letting the same students contribute most of the time. To make sure you're getting all students involved, begin by asking the student in the center of the room his / her opinion, and then work your way out.
- Make sure the discussion isn't losing steam. If it is, end it, even if you planned for it to last longer.
- Consider follow-up questions. Sometimes a discussion question generates a certain amount of discussion, but doesn't go any further. Be prepared with some additional questions to keep the conversation flowing.

Lesson 4
Student's Book p. 45

> ✓ **Homework Check!**
> Workbook pp. 135 and 136, Activities 1 and 2
> **Answers**
> **1 Look at the pictures and mark (✓) the sentences that might be true.**
> 1, 2
> **2 Read and rewrite the actions that Debbie had completed by the time her mom got home from work.**
> 1. Debbie had had breakfast. 2. Debbie had cleaned her room. 3. Debbie had taken a break. 4. Debbie had done her homework. 5. Debbie had picked up her little brother from camp. 6. Debbie had gone to the grocery store. 7. Debbie had started making dinner.

Warm-up
Students review past participles with a *Bingo* game.
- Draw a grid on the board with nine squares.
- Have students draw a similar grid and write the base form of verbs from the unit.
- Explain that you will say the past participles of the verbs. Students cross out the base forms of the verbs as they hear them.
- The first student who has crosses running horizontally, diagonally or vertically shouts *Bingo!* That student reads back the base form of the verb and the past participle.

Stop and Think! Critical Thinking
Is it a good idea to keep a pet in an apartment in the city? Is it the same for a dog, a cat, a goldfish or a hamster?
- Have students brainstorm different types of living arrangements: an apartment, a single-family home, etc.
- Ask students to share their living arrangements. Ask them if they have outdoor space, such as balconies or yards.
- Ask *Does anyone have a pet?* Elicit some answers.
- Then ask *Is it a good idea to keep a pet in an apartment or city? What kind of problems can occur? Does it matter what kind of pet it is?*
- Students form small groups to discuss.

4 Look at the sentences and answer the questions.
Students analyze sentences to understand the past perfect.
- Draw students' attention to the **The Past Perfect** box and explain how the tense is formed.

Answers
1. past, 2. 2, 1, 2, 1

5 Think Fast! Underline four more examples of the past perfect in WonderVet's reply to Jesse.
Students do a three-minute timed challenge: they identify examples of verbs in the past perfect in the e-mail in Activity 3.

Answers
1. hadn't gone, 2. had been, 3. hadn't done, 4. hadn't taught

6 Put the verb in parentheses in the past perfect.
Students complete the sentences in past perfect using the prompts.

Answers
1. had cleaned the closet out, 2. hadn't put her toys away, 3. had thrown it away, 4. hadn't taken the trash out, 5. had wiped it off, 6. hadn't hung my clothes up

Extension
Students role-play a vet and a client.
- Ask students the questions about pets:
  » *Do you have any pets? What kind?*
  » *Do you have any problems with your pets? If so, what kind?*
  » *Have you ever visited a vet for your pet's problems? What happened?*
- After discussing the questions as a class, have students count off by the letters *V* and *C*. The V students will be vets and the C students will be their clients.
- The clients meet in small groups to discuss what kinds of problems different pets have. They each decide which pet they own and what the problem is.
- The vets meet with each other in small groups to discuss treatment for various problems.
- Pair up a vet with a client. They act out their roles.
- Come together as a class and invite students to share their conversations.

Wrap-up
Students practice the past perfect with a game called *What Have You Done Lately?*
- As a class, brainstorm at least ten activities that students have done using past simple and time references, for example, *studied for the test, yesterday evening*.
- Students form small groups. They take turns telling their group mates something they completed before one of the listed activities, using the past perfect and a time word or phrase.
- As a class have some students share what they learned about their classmates.

⇒ **Workbook p. 136, Activity 3**

Listening & Speaking

Objective
Students will be able to identify key words while listening and to convince others orally.

Lesson 5   Student's Book pp. 46 and 47

> ✔ **Homework Check!**
> Workbook p. 136, Activity 3
> **Answers**
> **3 Look at the picture and complete the sentences with past the perfect.**
> 1. had gone, 2. had been, 3. had broken, 4. had hit, 5. had gotten

▶ 48 **Warm-up**
Students predict a reading from pictures and key words.
- Write the following words on the board: *large family, brothers, sisters, bedroom, chores, system*. (Leave these on the board for later.)
- Draw students' attention to the pictures on page 46. Ask *What do you think the listening will be about?*
- Students form small groups and predict the topic of the listening.
- Monitor, offering help as needed.
- Come together as a class and have some students share their predictions.

1 Discuss these questions.
- Students talk about their families and how they distribute the household chores in small groups in preparation for the activities that follow.
- Draw students' attention to the **Guess What!** box. Tell them on average, US mothers spend 18 hours on household chores every week. Fathers spend just 10 hours. Ask them how different it is in their families and communities.

2 **Listen to Carlton describing the household chores in his family. Circle T (True) or F (False).**
Students listen to Simone asking about Carlton's big family and circle *T* or *F*.
Answers
1. F (Carlton has four sisters and one brother.), 2. T, 3. F (Carlton shares a bedroom with his brother.), 4. T, 5. T, 6. F (His parents do not pay him.)

Audio Script
SIMONE: Carlton, do you come from a large family or a small one?
CARLTON: Ha ha! Simone, I come from a really large family!
SIMONE: How many brothers or sisters do you have?
CARLTON: I have four sisters and one brother.
SIMONE: Wow! Which one are you?
CARLTON: I'm number four. My brother is the oldest.
SIMONE: Are you happy to come from a large family?
CARLTON: Of course! I love my brother and sisters!
SIMONE: Are there bad things about it?
CARLTON: Yes, there are. I share a bedroom with my brother. I really want my own room.
SIMONE: Uh-huh.
CARLTON: We also do chores every week. With six children, my parents can't do everything.
SIMONE: I never do any chores.
CARLTON: You're lucky. Well, in my family, we have a special system to distribute the chores.
SIMONE: Do your parents pay you?
CARLTON: No! My parents don't pay us to do chores. We have another system…

Wrap-up
Students retell the content of a listening.
- Students form pairs. Draw their attention to Activity 2.
- Say *Correct the false statements*.
- When students have finished, draw their attention to the words on the board and the sentences in Activity 2.
- Using the words on the board and the information in Activity 2, they take turns retelling the content of the listening.
- Monitor, offering help as needed.

▶ **Workbook p. 137, Activity 1**

🎓 Teaching Tip
Managing Fast Finishers
Some students complete activities more quickly than others, so it's a good idea to have a few extra activities on hand, otherwise these students may become bored and disruptive. One set of activities designed for fast finishers are the **Just for Fun** pages. Students can work on these individually and then check their answers in the back of the Student's Book. The *Just for Fun* activities for this unit are on page 54.

Lesson 6   Student's Book p. 47

> ✔ **Homework Check!**
> Workbook p. 137, Activity 1
>
> **Answers**
> 1 Read the article. Then write *K* (Karla) or *J* (Jenessa).
> 1. K, 2. J, 3. K, 4. J

Warm-up

Students rate household chores to review vocabulary and generate interest.

- Draw students' attention to the pictures on page 46. Ask *What chores are they doing?*
- With the class, brainstorm other chores. Elicit the phrasal verbs on pages 42 and 43. Write them on the board.
- Have students rank the chores from 1 to 10, 1 being *not so bad* and 10 being *horrible*.
- Students form small groups and share their rankings.
- Take a vote on the most horrible chore.

3 🎧¹³ **The diagram shows how Carlton's family distributes the chores. Discuss how you think it works. Listen to check.**

Students guess how they think the color wheel could be used to distribute chores. Then they listen to the conversation and find out how the family does it.

Audio Script

SIMONE: What is your family's system?
CARLTON: We have a wheel on the fridge.
SIMONE: A wheel?
CARLTON: Yeah. In the middle, there are six colors.
SIMONE: OK.
CARLTON: On the outside, there are our names: Carlton, Kayla, Lizzie, Kevin, Grace and Ruth.
SIMONE: How does it work?
CARLTON: Every week, we move the wheel. The color shows your chore for the week.
SIMONE: So what are the chores?
CARLTON: Well, some are good and some are… just horrible.
SIMONE: Tell me.
CARLTON: OK. Yellow. That's OK. Yellow is walk the dog.
SIMONE: That's a nice chore!
CARLTON: Yeah, but blue… Blue is clean the bathroom.
SIMONE: What? Everything? Ew!
CARLTON: Green is take out the trash.
SIMONE: Green… take out the trash. I'm writing this down.
CARLTON: Orange is washing up after dinner.
SIMONE: Orange, washing up. So purple is…
CARLTON: Purple is drying up.
SIMONE: Drying up, and putting away the plates.
CARLTON: Exactly.
SIMONE: And red?
CARLTON: Red is helping out with the laundry.
SIMONE: Hanging up clothes… picking clothes up off the floor.
CARLTON: All of that. And there are six of us in my family, remember!
SIMONE: That's a lot of laundry.
CARLTON: Tell me about it!

4 **Listen again and complete the chores in each color of the wheel.**
- Draw students' attention to the ***Be Strategic!*** box and read the information aloud.
- Students complete the wheel with the keywords in each color.

Answers
1. walk the dog, 2. clean the bathroom, 3. take out the trash, 4. wash up, 5. dry up, 6. help out with laundry

5 **Think of all the chores that people do in your house: your parents, you and anybody else who lives with you. Put them in these groups.**
Students identify the chores and write the names of their family members who do each type of chore.

Answers
Answers will vary.

6 **Work in groups of six. Imagine you live together. Design your own wheel with six names and six chores.**
Students pretend they are a household and distribute chores using the system described in the listening. Students try to convince each other to trade chores if they are unhappy with the chores they got.

Wrap-up

Students compare and contrast the way their families distribute chores.

- Draw students' attention to the questions in Activity 1 on page 46.
- Students form small groups to compare and contrast how their families distribute chores.
- Come together as a class and ask students to say which way they think is most fair.

▶ **Workbook p. 137, Activities 2 and 3**

Preparing for the Next Lesson
Ask students to watch a video of the Songkran Festival in Thailand: https://goo.gl/HskerN or read about it: http://goo.gl/3nC8KF.

 Culture

Objectives
Students will be able to talk about the Songkran Festival in Thailand.

Lesson 7 Student's Book pp. 48 and 49

> ✔ Homework Check!
> Workbook p. 137, Activities 2 and 3
> Answers
> **2 Read the article again and answer the questions.**
> Answers will vary.
> **3 In your notebook, write your own opinion about the article.**
> Answers will vary.

 50

Warm-up
Students make a KWL Chart to preview the topic.
- Draw a KWL Chart on the board, similar to following:

What I Know	What I Want to Know	What I Have Learned

- Ask students to copy it in their notebooks and to answer the first two columns about Thailand.
- Tell students that they will fill in the third column at the end of the class.

1 🎧¹⁴ **Complete the missing words in the fact file on Thailand. Then listen and check.**
Students activate prior knowledge by completing the fact file. Then they listen to the audio to check their answers.
Answers
1. Asia, 2. capital, 3. million, 4. beaches, 5. flag

Audio Script
Thailand is a country in Southeast Asia. Its capital city is Bangkok. It has a population of about 68 million people. It is a hot country and it's very popular with tourists for its many beautiful beaches, such as the ones on the island of Koh Samui. The Thai flag is made of five stripes that are red, white and blue.

2 Read the text on the Songkran Festival in Thailand. Complete it with the missing sentences a–g (there is one extra).
Students read the text about the festival and determine where the missing sentences fit.
Answers
1. c, 2. f, 3. a, 4. e, 5. g, 6. b

3 Work in pairs to answer the questions.
Students form pairs and answer the questions based on the text.
Answers
Answers will vary.

Wrap-up
Students discuss their reactions to a text.
- Draw students' attention to the text in Activity 2 and the questions in Activity 3.
- Write the following questions on the board:
  » *Are there any similar festivals in your country? If so, describe them.*
  » *Have you ever been to the Songkran Festival?*
    ▪ *If so describe it.*
    ▪ *If not, would you like to go? Why or why not?*
- Students form small groups of three or four to discuss.
- Monitor, offering help as needed.
- Come together as a class and have some students share their thoughts and ideas.
- Ask students to fill in the third column of the KWL chart with what they have learned about Thailand.

➡ **(No homework today.)**

> **Teaching Tip**
> **Getting Students to Listen Closely**
> Listening is often a neglected skill. Try this to help your students become better listeners:
> - Say it just once. Repeating yourself in the classroom just trains students to become accustomed to hearing instructions more than once.
> - Create questions. If students are listening to a text, watching a video clip or hearing a story read aloud, break it up by stopping a few times and having students write a question or two about they heard. After the activity, pairs can quiz each other with their questions.

Lesson 8
Student's Book pp. 48 and 49

Warm-up
Students play a game of Broken Telephone to generate interest.
- Whisper a sentence about Thailand to a student, for example, "It is a hot country with many beaches that are popular with tourists." Make sure the other students can't hear.
- Indicate that the student should whisper what she has heard to the student next to her. Make sure students understand that they cannot repeat the sentence and must simply say what they have heard.
- When the last student has heard the sentence, ask him / her to say it aloud.
- Try to find out where the telephone "broke," that is, where the sentence was said or heard incorrectly.

4 Look at the pictures. Imagine the people below were at the Songkran Festival. In your notebook, write a comment for the blog on page 49 for each person. Were they happy or unhappy?

Students write comments for Krit, Sudarat, Bob and Tammy and their experience in the Songkran Festival for the blog on page 49.

Answers
Answers will vary.

5 Discuss these questions.
- In a personalization activity, students discuss the questions about how a water festival would be like in their hometowns.
- Draw students' attention to the **Guess What!** box. Tell them The old name of Thailand was Siam. The adjective is still used today in some cases, for example, Siamese cats.

Extension
Students research other water festivals.
- Ask students if they know of any other water festivals around the world.
- Elicit or provide the following and write them on the board: *Thingyan, Seattle Water Balloon Fight, Dai Water Splashing Festival, Fiesta del Agua y del Jamon, Chaul Cham Thmey, Vardavar, New York City Water Fight*.
- Have students choose or assign one of the festivals to research. Students can work individually or in groups.
- Tell students to answer these questions:
   » Where does the festival take place?
   » When does it take place?
   » How long does it last?
   » What does it celebrate?
   » When was it first celebrated?
- Have students present their research to the class. Encourage them to use visual aids, such as a Power Point presentation, photos or videos.

Wrap-up
Students discuss their KWL Charts.
- Students take out their KWL Charts from the previous lesson.
- Students form small groups of three or four and share what they have learned about Thailand.
- Encourage students to discuss some of the following questions:
   » What was the most interesting thing you learned?
   » What was the most surprising thing you learned?
   » Would you like to travel to Thailand? Why or why not?
- Monitor, offering help as needed.
- Come together as a class and have some students share their thoughts and ideas.

➡ **(No homework today.)**

Project

Objectives
Students will be able to use **household chores** and the **past perfect** vocabulary to write a scene from a play.

Lesson 9   Student's Book pp. 50 and 51

Warm-up
Students predict a listening text based on pictures.
- Draw students' attention to the pictures in Activity 2.
- Ask *What do you think the listening will be about?*
- Students form pairs to discuss.
- Have students share their thoughts and ideas. Don't focus on accuracy. Just let students express themselves.

1 Think Fast! How many words do you know for members of the family? Can you think of one relative that begins with the letters F, M, B, S, D, G, C, N, U and A?
Students do a two-minute timed challenge: they recall vocabulary for family relationships.

Answers
Possible answers: father, mother, brother, sister, daughter, grandmother, cousin, niece, uncle, aunt

2 Families often argue. Think of one reason for an argument:
Students brainstorm potential arguments families could have in different places or on different topics.

3 🎧¹⁵ Listen to the family. Answer the questions.
Students listen to the audio and identify where the family conflict takes place.

Answers
1. c, 2. the living room, 3. it always happens, 4. yes

Audio Script
DAD: Ryan! Madison! Where's the remote control? I want to watch TV.
RYAN: I don't know.
MADISON: Last night, when I went to bed, Mom had left it in the living room.
DAD: It's not here! It should be on the coffee table! Why can't you leave it in the same place?
MADISON: I'll help you look for it.
DAD: And look at the mess in this room! Comic books! Sweaters! I thought I had asked you to pick up your stuff.
MADISON: Come on, Dad! I can't clean up all the time.
DAD: It's not here. This always happens! Your mom told me she had asked you both to leave the remote in its place.
MADISON: Ask Ryan. The last time you looked for it, he had left it in the kitchen.
DAD: Ryan! Can you come and help us, please?
RYAN: I'm busy, Dad! I'm doing my homework.
MADISON: I see it! It's on the fridge!
DAD: What? Who put it there?
MADISON: Hey, Dad, it's not my fault. Don't blame me!
DAD: This family is crazy!

4 🎧¹⁵ Complete the conversation with the missing sentences a–e. Listen again to check.
Students identify where the missing sentences fit in the conversation and listen again to check their answers.

Answers
1. c, 2. e, 3. d, 4. b, 5. a

Wrap-up
Students express their opinions about a listening text.
- Write the following questions on the board:
  » *Do you think that the family should have argued? Why or why not?*
  » *Do you think the father was fair to say the family was crazy? Why or why not?*
  » *Do you think the children showed proper respect to their father? Why or why not?*
  » *Does your family ever argue over chores?*
- Students form pairs and discuss the questions.
- Monitor, offering help as needed.
- Come together as a class and have some students share their thoughts and ideas.

Lesson 10   Student's Book p. 51

Warm-up
Students review rooms with a game of Ten Questions.
- Model the game by telling students you are thinking of a room, for example, *kitchen*.
- Tell students they can ask you ten *yes / no* questions to find out the room.
- When students have guessed the room, have them form groups of four or five.
- Students take turns thinking of and trying to guess rooms.
- Monitor, offering help as needed.
- Rooms students can use for this activity include *living room, dining room, kitchen, bedroom, study, hall, bathroom, basement, porch, garage.*

5 Perform the dialogue in Activity 4. One person is Dad, one person is Ryan and one person is Madison.
Students form groups of three to perform the dialogue.

6 Work in small groups. Write a scene from a play.
Using the listening and the dialogue they performed in Activity 5 as a model, students write a scene from a play about a family argument and perform it for the class. Encourage them to use the past perfect.

The Digital Touch
To incorporate digital media in the project, suggest one or more of the following:
- Video-record your play with your smartphones or camera.
- Create a Power Point presentation to provide various background scenes for your play.

Note that students should have the option to write the scene on paper or digitally.

Extension
Students write dialogues based on three pictures.
- Draw students' attention to the pictures in Activity 2.
- Students form pairs and write dialogues similar to the one in Activity 4, based on one (or all) of the other three pictures.
- Have students practice the dialogues and present some of them to the class.

Wrap-up
Students vote on their plays.
- Write the following questions on the board:
  » Which play depicted the most believable scenario?
  » Which script was the best?
  » Which "actors" were the best?
  » Which dialogue was the best?
- After students have performed their plays, ask students to answer the questions, voting on the plays. Encourage to be respectful when they give feedback to their classmates.
- Give "awards" for the plays.

➡ **Workbook p. 136, Activity 1 (Review)**

Teaching Tip
Getting Students to Deal with Vocabulary Queries
There's a big difference between someone telling you something and learning something. Part of our role as teachers is to facilitate independent learning. When students ask questions, try these tips first before answering right away:
- When a student asks you to explain a word, don't. See if another student can explain it first.
- Put students in pairs or small groups and get them to explain the words they know to each other. The vocabulary one student knows will be different from the one others know.
- Sometimes the answer is right there in front of them. Encourage students to guess the meaning of words from context.
- Don't forget about dictionaries. The act of looking up a word in a dictionary results in higher retention than you simply telling students the definition.

Review

Objective
Students will be able to consolidate their understanding of **household chores** vocabulary and the **past perfect**.

Lesson 11   Student's Book p. 52

✔ **Homework Check!**
Workbook p. 136, Activity 1 (Review)

Answers
1 Complete the e-mail with the past perfect of the verbs in parentheses.
1. had taken out, 2. had wiped off, 3. had hung up, 4. had bought

▶ 54

Warm-up
Students review vocabulary with a football game.
- Draw the following football field on the board:

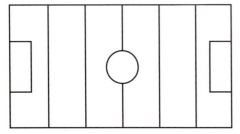

- Divide the class into two teams. Draw a symbol for Team A at one end of the field and another symbol for Team B.
- Flip a coin to see which team will be Team A and go first.
- Ask a student from Team A a review question or item (see below).
- If the student is correct, move his marker one space up the field. If not, a student from Team B gets a chance to answer it.
- Continue playing. When a team's marker gets to the last line before the goal, ask a question. If the student answers the question correctly, she "scores a goal."
- Play until you have covered all you want to review. The team with the most goals wins.
- Here are some items you can use in your review:
  » Please wipe ___ the table. (off)
  » Put ___ your games. (away)
  » Can you clean ___ the closet? (out)
  » Did you throw ___ my favorite shirt? (away)

1 Circle the correct option to complete the sentences.
Students review phrasal verbs by selecting the correct one in each sentence.

Answers
1. b, 2. c, 3. a, 4. c, 5. a, 6. b

2 🎧16 **Listen and complete the conversation.**
Students use the listening to complete the conversation with the correct phrasal verbs.

Answers
1. hang up, 2. cleaned up, 3. threw out, 4. picked up, 5. pick up, 6. clean up

Audio Script
A: Honey, can you hang these clothes up, please?
B: Sure, Mom. Err… Mom? Mom, why is my closet empty?
A: I cleaned it up this afternoon.
B: You did what? Where is my comic book collection? It was in the closet.
A: Oh, I threw those old comics out with the trash.
B: What? I had over a hundred comics in there! I'd collected them for years. I'm going to get them out of the trash can right now.
A: Ah, that will be difficult.
B: Why?
A: They picked the trash up this afternoon.
B: How could you do this to me? My comic collection! Lost!
A: Don't blame me. I tell you to pick your room up all the time and you never listen, so I did it.
B: My comic books are not trash!
A: They are now, dear. Now, help me clean the hall up before your father comes home.
B: The hall? Who cares about the hall? This is the worst day of my entire life!

3 Match the statements to the responses. There are two extra responses.
Students review phrasal verbs.

Answers
1. a, 2. e, 3. f, 4. b, 5. d, 6. g

Wrap-up
Students review phrasal verbs with a Memory game.
- Have students take out four pieces of paper and cut each into four pieces, making sixteen cards in total.
- Students write the two parts of each phrasal verb on separate cards: *clean out, take out, hang up, throw away, put away, pick up, wash up, wipe off*.
- Students form pairs and shuffle the cards. They lay them face-down between them. They take turns and play Memory.
- Students play until all pairs of cards are matched up. The student with more pairs wins.
- When students match two cards, challenge them to say use the phrasal verb in a sentence.

➡ **(No homework today.)**

Lesson 12   Student's Book p. 53

Warm-up

Students review past participles with a game of Tic Tac Toe.
- Draw a grid with nine squares on the board.
- Students draw a similar grid in their notebooks and write the base forms of the verbs from the unit randomly in the squares. Students should add one more verb of their choice.
- Students form pairs. One student is O and the other is X.
- Student O begins by saying the past participle of one of the verbs from the unit. If Student X has that base form, he / she puts an X over it.
- Then Student X says another verb from the unit and if Student O has that base form, he / she puts an X over it.
- The first student who has marked the verbs diagonally, horizontally or vertically says the base and past participle form of the verbs. If the student says them correctly, he / she wins.

4 Complete the sentences with the past perfect form of the verbs in parentheses.

Students review how to form the past perfect by completing sentences using the prompts.

Answers

1. hadn't washed, 2. hadn't reviewed, 3. had missed, 4. had had, 5. had lost, 6. hadn't eaten

5 Circle the correct options to complete the text.

Students select if the verbs in the past or the past perfect are correct to complete each sentence.

Answers

1. had gone, 2. returned, 3. had found, 4. copied, 5. had jumped, 6. hadn't waited

6 Correct the sentences.

Students identify the incorrect tense in each sentence.

Answers

1. will go Neil went to the dentist because he had lost a tooth. 2. die It hadn't rained for months, so all the plants in the garden died. 3. go We went to the supermarket because there wasn't any food in the fridge. 4. will sleep I fell asleep in class because I hadn't slept the night before. 5. will have We had had a problem in the bathroom and there was water everywhere!

Big Question

Students are given the opportunity to revisit the Big Question and reflect on it.
- Ask students to turn to the unit opener on page 41 and think about the question *How do you help at home?*
- Ask students to think about the discussions they've had on chores and responsibilities at home, the readings and the play they wrote.
- Students from small groups to discuss the following:
  » Do you receive an allowance (money paid for the chores you do)? If so, how much?
  » Do you think all kids should receive allowances, or is doing chores part of your responsibility as a family member? Explain.
  » Do you like to clean up your room? Why or why not?
  » Many people do a "spring cleaning," that is, do a big cleaning around springtime. Why do you think springtime makes people want to clean?
- Monitor, offering help as needed, particularly with vocabulary.

Scorecard

Hand out (and/or project) a *Scorecard*. Have students fill in their *Scorecards* for this unit.

➡ **Study for the unit test.**

4 Are you lucky?

Grammar	Vocabulary
Second Conditional: If I <u>broke</u> a mirror, I <u>would</u> have seven years of bad luck.	**Lucky Charms:** evil eye, fortune cat, fortune cookies, four-leafed clover, horse shoe, ladybug, rabbit's foot **Adverbs of Manner:** accidentally, badly, cleverly, deliberately, noisily, quickly, silently, slowly, stupidly, well

Reading	Writing
Identifying the author's audience and tone	Writing to a specific audience and giving advice

Are you lucky?

In the first lesson, read the unit title aloud and have students look carefully at the unit cover. Encourage them to think about the message in the picture. At the end of the unit, students will discuss the big question: *Are you lucky?*

Teaching Tip
Using Differentiated Instruction
Differentiated instruction helps you keep your students engaged by meeting their learning needs. Here are some tips:
- Get to know your students. Where does each student have trouble? What are each student's strengths? Consider this when you plan your lessons.
- Use flexible grouping. Group students by similar needs or interests, but change the groups often. Students can benefit by being with others at the same level, but sometimes they can improve by being with students who are more proficient.

Vocabulary

Objective
Students will be able to use **lucky charms** vocabulary and **adverbs of manner**.

Lesson 1
Student's Book pp. 56 and 57

Warm-up

Students discuss luck to activate prior knowledge and generate interest.
- Write the word *Lucky* on the board.
- Ask *Do you think you're lucky?* Elicit a few responses.
- Write the following questions on the board:
  » *Do you have any "lucky charms," something you carry that brings you good luck?*
  » *Are there any lucky colors or numbers?*
  » *Would you change your phone number to avoid "bad numbers"?*
  » *Do you believe some materials are lucky or unlucky (such as gold, silk, etc.)?*
- Students form small groups to discuss.
- Monitor, offering help as needed.
- Come together as a class and have some students share their thoughts and ideas.

1 Look at the pictures on pages 56 and 57. Write the correct numbers.
Students match the pictures with the superstitions vocabulary.

Answers

a. 7, b. 3, c. 6, d. 2, e. 1, f. 5, g. 4

2 Read and write the correct number that describes each picture.
Students are exposed to adverbs of manner as they match the descriptions with the illustrations.

Answers

1. d, 2. a, 3. e, 4. b, 5. c

3 Match the underlined words in Activity 2 with their opposites.
Students learn more adverbs of manner as they identify the antonyms of the adverbs in Activity 2.

Answers

1. badly, 2. slowly, 3. stupidly, 4. noisily, 5. accidentally

Extension
Students identify adverbs in their favorite books or stories to personalize the lesson.
- Have students bring in their favorite books or stories. You may wish to have some books on hand.
- Have students tell you what function an adverb has. Provide them with the following sentence and ask them to choose the correct answer or answers: *An adverb describes **a noun / a verb / an adjective / another adverb**.* (Answer: *An adverb describes **a verb / an adjective / another adverb**.*)
- Have students take out their books. Either individually or in pairs, students identify and list the adverbs they find in the books.
- Students form pairs and take turns pointing out what words the adverbs describe.
- Students take turns telling each other about their books, using the adverbs from their list.
- Monitor, offering help as needed.
- Come together as a class and have a few students tell the class about their books.

Wrap-up
Students practice adverbs with a game of *Go Fish*.
- Have each student take out a piece of paper and tear or cut it into ten pieces.
- On each piece, students write the adverbs from Activities 2 and 3.
- Students form groups of three or four.
- They put their cards together. One student shuffles the cards and deals out five cards to each student. The rest of the cards are spread out on the desk in between the students, making the "pond."
- The student to the left of the student who dealt asks the student to his left for the opposite of one of his cards. For example, if he has *well*, he asks, "Do you have *badly*?" If the student doesn't have the card, she says, "Go fish," and the first student chooses a card from the pond. If it matches, he continues playing by asking the next student for another opposite. If the student has the opposite, she gives it to the first student. The first student asks the next student for another opposite.
- Students play until all cards have been matched up. The student with the most pairs wins.

➡ **Workbook p. 138, Activities 1 and 2**

Lesson 2   Student's Book p. 57

✔ Homework Check!
Workbook p. 138, Activities 1 and 2
Answers
1 Label the pictures with the words in the box.
1. rabbit's foot, 2. four-leaf clover, 3. horseshoe,
4. ladybug, 5. evil eye, 6. fortune cookie
2 Match the underlined words or phrases to the correct adverbs with a similar meaning.
1. c, 2. a, 3. e, 4. b

Warm-up
Students rate good luck charms.
- Draw students' attention to the pictures on pages 56 and 57.
- Elicit the names of the good luck charms.
- Students form pairs and rate how lucky the items are. Encourage students to add their own ideas of what charms are lucky.
- Monitor, offering help as needed.
- Come together as a class and have some students share their thoughts and ideas.

4 ¹⁷ **Complete the sentences with the words from Activity 3. Then listen and check.**
Students practice the use of adverbs of manner by completing sentences.

Answers
1. slowly, 2. well, 3. deliberately, 4. quickly, 5. cleverly

Audio Script
1. One day, I saw a ladybug. I went toward it slowly so it didn't fly away and I took and amazing photo! The best of my life.
2. We won the school music competition! We practiced for months and we played really well on the day.
3. My sister says I deliberately broke her laptop, but I didn't! It was an accident! I spilled some soda.
4. We saw the bus and we ran quickly down the street and I fell down and broke my nose. It's the third time, so my sister gave me a rabbit's foot for good luck.
5. My grades are low in English class. I cleverly studied as much as I could and I got a better grade!

5 In pairs, read the sentences in Activities 2 and 4 again. Discuss which ones are accidents or related to the person's luck or effort.
Students discuss whether the situations described in Activities 2 and 4 were brought about by accident, luck or effort.

Answers
Answers will vary.

6 Think Fast! We make many adverbs by adding *–ly* to a verb, for example, *quick* → *quickly, happy* → *happily*. How many other adverbs can you make?
Students do a two-minute timed challenge: they see how many adverbs they can make by adding *–ly* to adjectives they already know.

Stop and Think! Critical Thinking
Do we make our own luck? Is it by effort or by accident?
- Draw students' attention to Activities 2 and 4. Ask them to say again which ones are accidents and which are related to a person's luck or effort.
- Ask *Do we make our own luck, or is it by effort or by accident?*
- Students form pairs and discuss.
- Come together as a class and have a few students share their thoughts and ideas.

Wrap-up
Students practice adverbs with a game.
- Students form pairs and take out one or two pieces of paper and tear or cut them into index-size pieces.
- Pairs write the adverbs from the lesson, as well as other adverbs they know, on the pieces of paper.
- One student shuffles the cards and places them in a pile.
- Students take turns turning over cards and making sentences with the adverbs.
- If a student makes a correct sentence, he / she keeps the card. The other student judges.
- Monitor, offering help as needed.
- The student with the most cards wins.

➡ **Workbook p. 138 and 139, Activities 3 and 4**

🐝 Teaching Tip
Using Ongoing Assessment
Here are a few tips for using ongoing, informal assessment:
- Have students draw you a picture of the concept.
- Have students summarize the concept in their own words.
- Assign a quick writing or speaking activity. Tell students to imagine a new student will be arriving tomorrow. *What would they tell her about today's lesson?*
- Have a weekly "quiz," ungraded. Tell students to use these as their own diagnostic tools to see where their weak points are.

# Grammar

Objective
Students will be able to use the **second conditional** to talk about luck.

Lesson 3   Student's Book pp. 58 and 59

✔ **Homework Check!**
Workbook p. 138 and 139, Activities 3 and 4
Answers
3 Underline the adverbs. Then write the correct adjective forms.
1. deliberately, deliberate, 2. silently, silent,
3. quickly, quick, 4. accidentally, accidental
4 Correct the mistakes.
1. ~~silently~~ badly, 2. ~~deliberately~~ quickly, 3. ~~quickly~~ noisily, 4. ~~badly~~ quickly

 Warm-up
Students practice using adverbs to prepare for the lesson with a game.
- Brainstorm as many adverbs as students can recall. This should be done at a quick pace.
- Draw students' attention to the pictures in Activity 1.
- Students form groups of three.
- Assign a random picture to the first group. You may wish to write the letters on pieces of paper and draw them from a bag.
- Tell them that they should describe what they see, using as many adverbs as they can as quickly as they can.
- Set a stopwatch for one minute.
- The first group describes the picture. Students can take turns or assign one person to speak. Keep track of how many adverbs they use as they describe the picture, awarding points for each and tallying them on the board.
- When the stopwatch goes off, assign a picture to the next group.
- Set the stopwatch, giving students one minute to describe the picture, as you keep tally on the board.
- Continue until all groups have described a picture. The group with the most points wins.

1 Look at the pictures with a partner. Discuss which ones are good or bad luck.
Students discuss the scenes in the illustrations and talk about whether each represents good or bad luck.
Answers
Answers will vary.

2 🎧¹⁸ Listen and number the pictures in the order you hear them.
Students listen to the situations that use the second conditional and they identify the order.

Answers
top to bottom, left to right 4, 2, 1, 5, 6, 3

Audio Script
1. GIRL: Oh my goodness. If I met Leo Messi, I wouldn't be able to say anything. I'd feel really shy. He's world famous!
2. GIRL: Oh come on! I wouldn't believe this message if it appeared on my screen and I certainly wouldn't click on any link. It would probably give your computer a virus.
3. BOY: If someone stole my bag, I'd ask an adult for help. I wouldn't run after the thief because it would be dangerous.
4. GIRL: How cool! If I saw the Loch Ness Monster, I would definitely take a photo of it! I'd be famous!
5. BOY: If I found $100 in the street, I wouldn't take it. It's not mine. That's a lot of money.
6. BOY: If a snail fell out of my bag of salad, I'd wash it and eat it anyway. It doesn't bother me!

3 Listen again and complete the sentences.
Using the verbs from the listening, students complete the second conditional sentences.
Answers
1. met, 2. believe, 3. ask, 4. saw, 5. found, 6. wash

4 Look at the sentences in Activity 3 and answer the questions.
Students identify features of the second conditional by examining example sentences in Activity 3.
- Draw students' attention to the **Second Conditional** box and read the information aloud.

Answers
1. hypothetical, 2. past simple, 3. would + verb in the base form

Wrap-up
Students practice the second conditional with a game called Catch.
- Bring a soft ball or crumple up a piece of paper to make a ball.
- Toss the ball to a student and say the first part of a second conditional sentence, for example, *If a black cat crossed my path…* The student should finish the sentence.
- That student then tosses the ball to another student and says the first part of a second conditional sentence. That student finishes it.
- Continue as long as time permits.

▶ **Workbook p. 139, Activities 1 and 2**

Lesson 4 — Student's Book p. 59

> ✔ **Homework Check!**
> Workbook p. 139, Activities 1 and 2
> **Answers**
> **1 Write commas (,) where needed.**
> 1. none, 2. none, 3. quickly, I, 4. foot,
> **2 Match the sentence halves.**
> 1. d, 2. e, 3. b, 4. a

Warm-up

Students practice the second conditional with a game called *Consequence Chain*.
- Say a sentence about yourself, for example, *If I didn't have this class right now, I'd still be in bed.*
- A student makes a sentence with consequence, for example, *If I were still in bed, I wouldn't learn about the second conditional.*
- The next student uses the consequence to make a second conditional sentence.
- Continue until all students have made a sentence. You may also do this activity in two or three groups.

5 Match the sentence halves.

Students match the beginnings and endings of second conditional sentences.
- Draw students' attention to the **Guess What!** box. Tell them we use a comma in the first part of the sentence when it starts with *if*.
- Ask students *Why do all the sentences have commas?* Because they start with the *if* clause.

Answers
1. c, 2. f, 3. e, 4. a, 5. d, 6. b

6 In your notebook, change the sentences in Activity 5 so they are true for you.

Students rewrite the second halves of the sentences using their own ideas.

Answers
Answers will vary.

7 Use the prompts to make second conditional sentences. Then compare with a partner.

Students use the cues to create the *if* clause of second conditional sentences and complete them with their own ideas.

Answers
Answers will vary.

Wrap-up

Students practice second conditional with a game called Going Away.
- Tell students to imagine that they are going away from home for one year. Ask *How would you spend your last day before you leave?*
- Write the following questions on the board:
  » *What special food would you want eat?*
  » *Who would you want to see?*
  » *What places would you go to?*
  » *What things would you do?*
- Students write answers to the questions about what they would do.
- Students form pairs and interview each other using the questions on the board. They write down their partner's answers using the third person.
- Monitor, offering help as needed.
- Come together as a class and have some students share what they learned about their classmates.

▶ **Workbook p. 139 and 140, Activities 3 and 4**

> 💭 **Teaching Tip**
> **Praising Students in the Classroom**
> It's important to give feedback to our students, but often we find it in the form of correction. Even when we present it positively, we often overlook actual praise. Be watchful for opportunities to praise behavior. In order for praise to be effective, it must seem spontaneous and genuine. Here are some tips:
> - Following directions. After you've explained how to do a task, keep an eye out for students who follow your directions as they proceed. Praise those students for being so attentive.
> - Being neat. As an activity progresses, go from student to student praising those students who maintain organization and neatness.
> - Taking calculated risks. Some students will try for a more creative approach to their work. Even if it's not exactly what you expected from them, praise those students for their creativity and willingness to "go out on a limb."
> - Task completion. Go from desk to desk or table to table, offering appropriate praise for one student and then for the next. Don't reserve praise for only high grades or a finished product. Praise is appropriate for any behavior that contributes to successful completion.

Reading & Writing

Objectives
Students will be able to identify the author's audience and tone. They will also be able to write to a specific audience and give advice.

Lesson 5   Student's Book p. 60

✔ **Homework Check!**
Workbook pp. 139 and 140, Activities 3 and 4

Answers
3 Complete the second conditional sentences with the correct form of the words in parentheses.
1. won, wouldn't be, 2. would be, said, 3. broke, would have, 4. gave, wouldn't have
4 Use the prompts to make second conditional sentences that are true for you.
Answers will vary.

Warm-up
Students prepare for the lesson with a *Chain Story*.
- Students take out a piece of paper each and write the first sentence or two of a story that tells about good or bad luck.
- Set a stopwatch for one minute.
- When the stopwatch goes off, say *Switch!* Students then put their pens down and pass the papers. They cannot finish their sentences once the stopwatch goes off.
- Students continue writing their story in the new piece of paper for another minute until you say *Switch!*
- Continue for about ten minutes or as long as students are engaged. Be sure you tell students when it's the final minute. Then they need to write an ending for their stories.
- Have some students read the stories aloud.
- Extend the activity by having students try to edit each other's writing and correct spelling errors.

1 Read Molly's e-mail and answer the questions.
Students read the text and answer comprehension questions.

Answers
1. basketball, 2. Her team always loses. 3. to ask her aunt for help, 4. informal

2 Read the reply and circle T (True) or F (False).
Students read the reply to the first e-mail and determine whether the statements about the text are true or false.

Answers
1. F (You cannot change what the other teams do.), 2. F (She also mentions golf.), 3. T, 4. T (In her opinion, we can make our own luck.), 5. F (She says that if she were two meters taller, life would have been easier.), 6. F (If she were Molly's age, she'd be very happy to play basketball with such good friends every week.)

Wrap-up
Students discuss an e-mail to personalize the activity and consolidate the lesson.
- Draw students' attention to the e-mail in Activity 1.
- Ask *Have you ever felt like Molly about sports or another activity? What happened in the end?* Elicit some responses.
- Students form groups of three to discuss.
- Monitor, offering help as needed.

➡ **Workbook pp. 140 and 141, Activities 1–3**

 Teaching Tip

Using Pre-Reading Strategies to Increase Comprehension
Before reading a selection aloud or before students read a text, try taking seven to ten minutes to build word and background knowledge. Decide how you might best make the concepts relevant and accessible to all of your students. This might be through a film, discussion, a game or a text read by you. Here are some strategies:
- Do motivating activities. Use any activity that gets students interested in the text and motivates them to read it. For example, you can send students a short e-mail before class.
- Build text-specific knowledge. Activate students' prior knowledge of a topic so they can use it as they read the text. For example, you can point greetings and closings out in your e-mail.
- Relate to students' lives. This is a powerful way to motivate students to read and help them understand what they will be reading. Before reading an e-mail from someone who is feeling unlucky, for example, ask students to reflect on a time that they felt unlucky.

Lesson 6   Student's Book p. 61

> ✔ Homework Check!
> Workbook pp. 140 and 141, Activities 1–3
>
> Answers
> **1 Read the article about superstitions.**
> **2 Read the article again and write the correct number of the superstition.**
> *left to right, top to bottom* 4, 3, 2, 1
> **3 Read the article again and circle *T* (True) or *F* (False).**
> 1. F, 2. F, 3. T, 4. T

Warm-up
Students express an opinion about an e-mail to prepare for the lesson.
- Draw students' attention to the e-mail in Activity 2.
- Ask *Do you think that Molly's Aunt Judy responded well? What's the best piece of advice she gave Molly?*
- Students form groups of three to discuss.
- Monitor, offering help as needed.
- Come together as a class and have some students share their thoughts and ideas.

3 Look again at Aunt Judy's e-mail. Write four suggestions that she makes.

Students reread the text in Activity 2 and identify four suggestions Aunt Judy gave.

Answers
1. If I were you, I wouldn't worry about the other teams. 2. Your team should practice hard. 3. The most important thing is to never give up. 4. One more thing is to stay positive.

4 Read Molly and Judy's e-mails again. Write the following information.

Students identify some writing conventions of informal writing in the e-mails on page 60.

Answers
1. Hi, Hello, 2. How are you? I'm fine, thanks! 3. I'm, We're, You're, etc. 4. See you soon, Speak soon

5 Read Logan's e-mail. In your notebook, write him a reply. Give him some advice.

Students read the e-mail, identify the problem expressed and write a reply giving Logan some advice.
- Draw students' attention to the **Be Strategic!** box and read the information aloud.
- Tell them to read the e-mail and ask *Is it an informal or formal e-mail? Informal.*
- Ask them to reply to Logan giving him some advice.

Answers
Answers will vary.

Extension
Students put the parts of an e-mail in the correct order.
- Before the lesson, make copies of either one of or all of the three e-mails on pages 60 and 61. Alternatively, find an authentic e-mail and print it out.
- Make copies of the e-mails(s), enough for each group of three students. Be sure to separate the greeting, closing and ideas in the body.
- Students form groups of three.
- Give sets of the e-mail(s) out to each group.
- Students race to put the e-mails in order.
- The first group to put the e-mail(s) in the correct order wins.

Wrap-up
Students write and respond to e-mails to consolidate the lesson.
- Draw students' attention to the e-mails on pages 60 and 61.
- Remind them of the Wrap-up question in Lesson 5, *Have you ever felt like Molly about sports or another activity?*
- Say *You will write an e-mail about a time when you felt unlucky.*
- Students write an e-mail, using Molly's as a model.
- Monitor, offering help as needed.
- When students have finished, collect the e-mails and redistribute them.
- Using Aunt Judy's e-mail as a model, students write responses to their classmates' e-mails.
- Monitor, offering help as needed.
- Collect the original e-mails and response e-mails and distribute them to their owners.
- Come together as a class and have some students share the advice they received. Encourage students to give their opinions of the advice.

▶ Workbook p. 141, Activity 4

Preparing for the Next Lesson
Ask students to watch an introduction to the Roman Empire: https://goo.gl/7PKUdk.

Culture

Objective
Students will be able to identify general facts about the Roman Empire.

Lesson 7 — Student's Book p. 62

> ✔ Homework Check!
> Workbook p. 141, Activity 4
> **Answers**
> **4 In your notebook, write an opinion essay about superstitions. Follow the guidelines below.**
> Answers will vary.

Warm-up
Students make a KWL Chart to preview the topic.
- Draw a KWL Chart on the board, similar to following:

What I Know	What I Want to Know	What I Have Learned

- Ask students to copy it and complete the first two columns.
- Tell students that they will read about Rome.

1 Think Fast! Name as many gods as you can. You could choose gods from any mythology (Roman, Greek, Aztec, etc.). Hint: think of the names of planets.
Students do a three-minute timed challenge: they brainstorm the names of gods from any civilization.

Answers
Answers will vary.

2 Read the short history of the Roman Empire. Then answer the questions.
Students read the article and identify two pieces of information.

Answers
1. worship of many gods, 2. Christianity

3 Read the text in Activity 2 again. Make a list of the gods mentioned.
Students reread the article and identify items in a category of information (gods).

Answers
Jupiter, Juno, Apollo, Venus, Julius Caesar

Extension
Students learn Roman numerals.
- Using a cross-curricular approach, introduce or review Roman numerals:

  I=1, II=2, III=3, IV=4, V=5, VI=6, VII=7, VIII=8, IX=9, X=10, XI=11 ... XX=20, XXX=30, XL=40, L=50, LX=60, LXX=70, LXXX=80, XC=90, C=100, D=500, M=1,000

- Help students to write their ages, the day they were born, the present day of week, their class numbers, etc.
- Students form pairs and quiz each other on numbers. For example, one student says *Three hundred forty-two*. The other student writes out the Roman numeral: *CCCXLII*.
- Monitor, offering help as needed.

Wrap-up
Students discuss Roman gods to consolidate the lesson.
- Brainstorm the names of the Roman gods and write them on the board.
- Write the following questions on the board:
  » Why do you think the Romans had so many gods?
  » How do you think they kept track of them all?
  » Why do you think Christianity became popular?
  » Do you see any parallels between Christianity and Greek gods?
- Students form groups of three and discuss.
- Monitor, offering help as needed.
- Come together as a class and have some students share their thoughts and ideas.

➡ **(No homework today.)**

Lesson 8   Student's Book pp. 62 and 63

Warm-up
Students review Roman gods with a game of *Hangman*.
- Draw a hangman's noose, like this, on the board:

- Choose one of the gods from the text, for example, *Jupiter*, and write the same number of blanks as there are in the word on the board:

__ __ __ __ __ __ __

- Students form two or three teams. Team members take turns calling out letters. If a student calls out a letter that is part of the word, for example, *t*, write that letter in the appropriate blank or blanks. If it is not part of the word, draw the person on the noose, beginning with the head. Draw one part of the body for each letter called that is not part of the word. Be sure to write the called-out letter to the side so that students don't call it out again.
- The game is over when teams have either guessed the word, completed the word, or the body is complete.
- If time permits, have a student come up and choose the name of a god, while others call out letters and try to guess. Award points for correct guesses.

4 🎧¹⁹ **Complete the text with the missing sentences. There is one extra. Then listen to check your answers.**
Students read the article and identify the most logical place for each sentence to be added.

Answers
1. c, 2. d, 3. b

Audio Script
Strange Gods of Rome
Fortuna was the goddess of luck. People still talk about "Lady Luck" today. There is often a piece of material over her eyes. This is because luck is blind. She also has the wheel of fortune. The wheel moves. When you are on top, you are lucky and happy. When you are at the bottom, you are unlucky and very unhappy!
Janus was the god of the beginning and the end. He has two faces. One looks back into the past and one looks into the future. The month January gets its name from this god because it is the end of one year and the start of the next.
Like Julius Caesar, Augustus was a real person, but the Romans worshipped him like a god. He was emperor for a long time 27 BC–14 AD (41 years). After he died, they built temples in his memory. The Romans named our modern month August after him, and they named July after Julius Caesar.

5 **Label the pictures with the correct names of the gods in Activity 4.**
Students apply information from the article on page 62 to determine the god each statue is of.

Answers
1. Janus, 2. Augustus, 3. Fortuna

6 **Look at the pictures of the god Atlas. Discuss the questions with a partner.**
Students infer and discuss information about another Roman god from the sculpture.

7 🎧²⁰ **Listen and check your answers.**
Students listen to the information about Atlas and check their ideas from the previous activity.

Audio Script
Atlas is a god from Ancient Greece and Rome. In this picture, he is carrying the whole world on his shoulders. Today, we use his name for the modern Atlas. This is a book with maps of the whole planet. Atlas carried planet Earth, and so the book takes his name.

Stop and Think! Critical Thinking
How are good and bad luck represented in your country? Is there a symbol for each one? Are they different from other countries?
- As a class, discuss what elements or customs represent good and bad luck in their community and also in their country.

Wrap-up
Students complete their KWL Charts.
- Students take out their KWL Charts from the previous lesson and complete the final column.
- Students form small groups of three or four and share what they have learned.
- Encourage students to discuss these questions:
  » *What was the most surprising thing you learned?*
  » *Would you like to have lived in ancient Rome? Why or why not?*
- Come together as a class and have some students share their ideas.

➡ **(No homework today.)**

 **Project**

> **Objective**
> Students will be able to create a poster about **superstitions**.

Lesson 9   Student's Book pp. 64 and 65

Warm-up

Students preview superstitions to generate interest and activate prior knowledge.
- Write or draw some images that represent superstitions, for example, *a black cat, 4, a broken mirror, 13, a crow flying overhead, an owl, an empty bucket, a horseshoe.*
- Ask *What do you think of when you see these words or images?*
- Students form pairs to discuss.
- Come together as a class and have some students share their ideas.
- Have students research them.

1 Read the dictionary definitions. Discuss common superstitions in your country with a partner.
Students read the definitions and talk about superstitions they are familiar with.

2 **Look at the poster of a popular superstition. Listen and complete the sentences.**
Students complete the sentences on the poster with words from the listening.
- Draw students' attention to the **Guess What!** box. Tell them that the hashtag # is not just for tweets. It also means number in American English: #14 = number fourteen.

Answers

1. both, 2. Germany, 3. magic, 4. home, 5. Japan, 6. pet

Audio Script

ERNIE: We're looking at superstitions around the world. Number 1, the Black Cat. Is it good luck or bad luck, Phoebe?
PHOEBE: That's the question, Ernie! Black cats bring both good luck and bad luck, depending on the country!
ERNIE: Where are they unlucky?
PHOEBE: All over Europe, people think black cats bring bad luck, especially in Germany.
ERNIE: Why is that?
PHOEBE: It's because black cats often accompany witches in old stories. People saw cats as symbols of black magic.
ERNIE: What nonsense! People will believe anything, won't they?
PHOEBE: That's true.
ERNIE: So are black cats bad luck everywhere?
PHOEBE: No. The exception is Britain. In Scotland, people think black cats are lucky, especially when one comes to your home.
ERNIE: Some good news for cats! What about outside of Europe?
PHOEBE: Cats are also good luck in Japan. If a black cat walks across your path, you can control your own luck!
ERNIE: I'm pleased to hear that. So do black cats still have a bad reputation?
PHOEBE: Yes, they do, Ernie. The cruel superstitions about black cats cause problems today. Many people don't want a black cat as a pet. Some 70% of cats without a home are black cats.
ERNIE: That's so silly!
PHOEBE: It happens, Ernie, and it's sad.

3 Read the poster again. Circle T (True) or F (False).
Students identify true and false statements about the information on the poster.

Answers

1. F (Scottish people think cats bring good luck when they come into your house.), 2. F (In Scotland, people think black cats are lucky.), 3. T, 4. T, 5. T

Stop and Think! Critical Thinking

In many countries, people think Friday the 13th is unlucky. Is this the same in your country?
- Show a calendar. Find a date where the 13th falls on a Friday.
- Ask *Why do people think Friday 13th is unlucky?* Elicit some answers.
- Ask *Is this the same in your country?*
- Elicit an answer and allow students to share their thoughts.

Wrap-up

Students play a game of *Two Truths and a Lie* to consolidate the lesson.
- Say three superstitions, two are true and one is a lie, for example:
  » *If a friend gives you a knife, you should give him a coin.* (True.)
  » *It's good luck to open an umbrella in the house.* (False. it's bad luck.)
  » *It's bad luck to walk under a ladder.* (True.)
- Students guess which one is the lie.
- Students write out three superstitions, two that are true and one that is a lie.
- Students play the game in small groups, trying to guess which is the lie.
- Play as long as time allows or as long as students are engaged.

Lesson 10 — Student's Book pp. 64 and 65

Warm-up

Students brainstorm superstitions to prepare for the lesson.
- Have students close their books.
- Set a stopwatch for two minutes.
- Students form pairs and brainstorm all the superstitions they know.
- Students take turns reading their superstitions aloud. As each superstition is read aloud, students cross it off their list if they have it.
- When all superstitions have been read, the pair with the most wins.

◀ **Work in small groups. Create a poster for "Superstitions Around the World."**

Students use the model poster and follow the steps to research and create their own posters about superstitions.

The Digital Touch

To incorporate digital media in the project, suggest one or more of the following:
- Get some guidance on using Power Point to make your poster: https://goo.gl/fELDoX.
- Here are some tips for designing posters with photos: https://goo.gl/oDTDdK.

Note that students should have the option to do a task on paper or digitally.

Extension

Students present their posters to their classmates.
- Draw students' attention to the questions in Step 2 of Activity 4.
- Have students bring their posters to the front of the class and explain why they chose the superstition, as well as answer the questions in Step 2.
- Encourage students to ask the student presenting questions about their superstition.

Wrap-up

Students vote on the best posters to consolidate the lesson.
- Have students display their posters, without showing their names. Assign each poster a number.
- Decide on some categories for students to vote on, for example:
  » Most interesting superstition
  » Most unusual superstition
  » Most attractive design
  » Best written copy
- Write the categories on the board. Students copy them onto a piece of paper.
- Students walk around and decide which poster wins in each category.
- After students have finished, tally the votes. Have the winners stand by their posters as the rest of the class applauds.

 **Workbook p. 140, Activity 1 (Review)**

Teaching Tip

Promoting Creativity in the Classroom

Encouraging your students to think more creatively is not only so that they are more engaged and have more fun; there is a growing belief that a fast-paced global economy requires workers with the flexibility of mind to adapt to change rather than follow a traditional career path. Here are ways you foster creativity:

- Create a classroom that recognizes creativity. You can design awards or bulletin boards to showcase different ways of solving problems or creative solutions to a real-world situation.
- Use the most effective strategies. Find out what works best with your students: consider using creative arts or media-oriented programs.
- Think of creativity as a skill. Begin each lesson with a problem to solve or question for students to consider. Leave it open-ended sometimes.
- Make emotional connections. Remember what you know about your students and tie in your lessons to what is meaningful to them.
- Be open to other discussions. You know that student who often asks the question that goes a little outside of the lesson? Don't shut him / her down, engage them. Validate their creativity.
- Reward students for thinking of problems in unconventional ways.

 Review

Objectives
Students will be able to consolidate their understanding of **lucky charms** and **adverbs of manner** vocabulary as well as the **second conditional**.

Lesson 11 Student's Book p. 66

✔ Homework Check!
Workbook p. 140, Activity 1
Answers
1 Complete the second conditional sentences.
Answers will vary.

Warm-up

 Students practice forming adverbs with a game of *Charades*.
- Students take out pieces of paper and cut them up or tear them up into 10 index-size pieces.
- Students form groups of three or four. They combine their cards and place them face-down on the desk.
- The first student takes a card and acts out a verb of her choice. She must include the adverb into her acting. For example, if she chooses *angrily*, she can act out any verb, but she must act it out in an angry manner.
- The student who guesses the adverb correctly keeps the card.
- Students continue to act out verbs and adverbs as time permits.
- The student with most cards wins.

1 Find ten adverbs in the word search.
Students identify adverbs of manner in the word search.

```
A N G R I L Y X H G
N I C E L Y Q W A X
Z B J G W P T L P N
D K T U M Z K A P O
N E W L Y H K Z I I
Q Q G A S J R I L S
W S T R O N G L Y I
U X X L Z W Q Y J L
J U K Y S A D L Y Y
Z S U D D E N L Y X
```

2 Complete the sentences with the adverb form of the adjective in parentheses.
Students form adverbs of manner and use them to complete the sentences.
Answers
1. accidentally, 2. badly, 3. quickly, 4. deliberately, 5. slowly

3 Cross out the wrong word in each sentence.
Students identify the adverb that does not fit in each sentence.
Answers
1. accidentally, 2. newly, 3. accidentally, 4. cleverly, 5. noisily, 6. stupidly, 7. quickly, 8. badly

4 Write sentences to describe each picture. Use adverbs from Activity 3.
Students describe each picture in a full sentence using an appropriate adverb from the previous activity in each.
Answers
1. He runs quickly. 2. He plays the drums noisily. 3. He works cleverly.

Extension
Students make original sentences using adverbs.
- Draw students' attention to the adverbs in Activity 1.
- Students form pairs.
- Set a stopwatch for two minutes.
- Pairs make as many sentences as they can in two minutes.
- When the stopwatch goes off, students put their pens down.
- Pairs take turns reading their sentences aloud. If they are correct, they get a point.
- The pair with the most points wins.

Wrap-up
Students practice adverbs with a game of Bingo.
- Draw a grid on the board with nine squares.
- Have students draw a similar grid on a piece of paper.
- Have them write nine adverbs from the unit in the grid.
- Say the adjective forms of the adjectives. If a student has the adverb form, they cross out the adjective.
- The first student to cross out three adverbs, either horizontally, diagonally or vertically, shouts *Bingo!*
- The student reads back the adverbs. Challenge the student to use each in a sentence.

▶ **(No homework today.)**

Lesson 12   Student's Book p. 67

Warm-up

Students guess information about their classmates to practice the second conditional.

- Have students write their names on a piece of paper and fold it up. They then drop it in a bag or box.
- Write the following sentence starters on the board:
  » *If you had to learn another language, I think you'd choose…*
  » *If you had a new car, I think you'd buy …*
  » *If you had a pet, I think you'd get a …*
  » *If you won the lottery, I think you'd …*
  » *If you got a job, I think you'd be a …*
  » *If you were an animal, I think you'd be a …*
  » *If you won a trip around the world for two, I think you'd take …*
  » *If you had more money, I think you'd buy …*
  » *If you had a super power, I think you'd choose to be able to …*
  » *If you did a new sport, I think you'd like to …*
- Go around the room, having each student draw a name from the bag.
- Students complete the sentences, making guesses about the student whose name they drew.
- When students have finished, they interview the student they guessed about.
- Come together as a class and have some students share what they thought about their classmate and what was actually true.

5 Match the sentence halves.

Students match the beginnings and endings of second conditional sentences.

Answers
1. d, 2. a, 3. f, 4. c, 5. e, 6. b

6 Complete the sentences with the correct form of the words in parentheses. Then listen and check.

Using the prompts, students complete the second conditional sentences with the correct form of each verb.

Answers
1. would be, 2. would get, 3. would take, 4. went, 5. wore, 6. wouldn't have, 7. saw, 8. wouldn't enjoy

Audio Script

MADISON: If I were a famous actor, I would be so happy! What a life!
DYLAN: What a life? You would get really stressed if you were famous.
MADISON: Why?
DYLAN: Every time you left your house, photographers would take your photo. If you went to the store, people would follow you everywhere.
MADISON: If I wore a hat and sunglasses, nobody would recognize me.
DYLAN: You can't wear sunglasses all the time! If you lived in the same house as now, you wouldn't have any privacy. If anyone saw you in the street, they would ask for a selfie. Imagine thousands of people around you with their smartphones.
MADISON: What are you saying, Dylan?
DYLAN: You wouldn't enjoy life if you were famous. It's a dream. It's not real life.
MADISON: Speak for yourself! Luck is on my side and I want to be a star!

7 Complete the sentences about you.

Students compose the consequence halves of second conditional sentences with their own ideas.

Answers
Answers will vary.

Big Question

Students are given the opportunity to revisit the Big Question and reflect on it.

- Ask students to turn to the unit opener on page 55 and think about the question *Are you lucky?*
- Ask students to think about the discussions they've had on luck, the readings they've read, the texts they've listened to and the poster they made.
- Students form small groups to discuss the following:
  » *Do you believe in luck? Why or why not?*
  » *Are there some cultures that are more superstitious or concerned with luck than others? Why do think this is?*
  » *Do you believe in superstitions? Why or why not?*
  » *Many people observe superstitions even when they don't believe in them. Why do you think this is?*
- Monitor, offering help as needed, particularly with vocabulary.

Scorecard

Hand out (and/or project) a *Scorecard*. Have students fill in their *Scorecards* for this unit.

➠ **Study for the unit test.**

5 Where would you rather go?

Grammar	Vocabulary
Preferences (+,-,?): I would like to stay in that hotel. I would prefer to eat in a restaurant. I would rather stay at home today. **Intensifiers (+,-,?):** These bags are too heavy. I'm not strong enough to pick this suitcase up.	**Air Travel:** boarding pass, booking a flight, customs, luggage, passport, visa stamp **Human-made Wonders:** Angkor Wat, Colosseum, Blue Mosque, Machu Picchu, Great Wall of China, Moai statues, Ponte Vecchio, Pyramid of Giza

Listening	Writing
Inferring relationships between events	Using past forms to write a narrative

Where would you rather go?

In the first lesson, read the unit title aloud and have students look carefully at the unit cover. Encourage them to think about the message in the picture. At the end of the unit, students will discuss the big question: *Where would you rather go?*

Teaching Tip
Starting Lessons with Brainstorming
Brainstorming taps into your students' prior knowledge. Try these with your students:
- Image brainstorm: Project an image related to your lesson onto a projector and ask students to tell you everything they can about the picture.
- ABC brainstorming. Students work in groups and try to come up with a word or phrase related to the topic that starts with every letter of the alphabet.
- Class brainstorm web. Write a word or phrase in a circle on the board. Students write as many words connected to it as they can think of. Use a stopwatch to liven it up.

Vocabulary

Objective
Students will be able to use **air travel** and **human-made wonders** vocabulary to write a post about a place they visited.

Lesson 1 Student's Book p. 70

Warm-up
Students play a guessing game to activate prior knowledge and generate interest.
- Hold up your book and point to each landmark on the unit opener on page 69, numbering them from left to right. Do not say the names of or other information about the landmarks.
- Have each student take out a piece of paper and write what they know about each landmark.
- Set a stopwatch for two or three minutes to liven up the activity.
- When students have finished, or the stopwatch goes off, have students mingle, asking and answering questions to find out about the landmarks.
- When students have shared all the information they can, come together as a class. Have students tell you what they know and found out about the famous landmarks.

1 Number the pictures.
Students identify air travel vocabulary words.

Answers

1. a, 2. e, 3. c, 4. d, 5. b

2 **²³ Look at the stages of traveling by plane. Number them in the order they happen. Then listen and check.**
Students look at the photos and read the captions. They number the steps in order and listen to the audio to check their answers.

Answers

left to right, top to bottom 7, 6, 9, 4, 1, 5, 3, 10, 2, 8

Audio Script
1. You book your flights.
2. You print out your boarding pass.
3. You arrive at the airport.
4. You check in your luggage.
5. You go through passport control.
6. You board the plane.
7. The plane takes off.
8. You land at your destination.
9 You pick up your suitcases at baggage claim.
10. You go through customs.

---

3 Close your books. Write down in order the stages of traveling by plane.
Students try to recall the order and target language from Activity 2.

- Have students close their books and list the steps for air travel. Check answers as a class.
- Draw students' attention to the **Guess What!** box. Tell them that the longest nonstop flight in the world is 13,800 kilometers long between Dubai and Panama City. It takes 17 and a half hours!

Stop and Think! Critical Thinking
Do you need a visa to go to the US or anywhere else? What are the steps to get a visa?
- Ask students to answer the question about the US and in what other countries they need a visa.
- Ask students who have a visa for another country to raise their hands. Elicit the names of the countries. Ask volunteers to share their experience getting one.

Extension
Students review vocabulary with a role play.
- Draw students' attention to the photos in Activities 1 and 2.
- Ask *Who are some of the people that you meet at those different stages?* Elicit or provide the following people and write them on the board: *a travel agent, an airline attendant, a traveler / passenger, a baggage handler, a immigration officer, the pilot, a customs inspector.*
- Tell students they will be role-playing people in an airport.
- Count students off by seven.
- Assign one role for each number.
- Students meet in groups according to their role and decide how their roles will act, what kind of situations their role will be in and what they will say.
- Have one student from each group meet with others from each group. Begin by asking the traveler where he / she is going and what's the first thing he / she has to do.
- Monitor and offer help as needed.

Wrap-up
Students review vocabulary with a game of Guess that Phrase.
- Draw students' attention to the stages of traveling by plane in Activity 2.
- Students form pairs and face each other.
- Explain that one student will describe a stage for his partner. If the partner guesses correctly, the pair awards themselves a point. If the partner can't guess, the first student can move on to another phrase and describes that.
- Set a stopwatch for five minutes.
- The pair with the most points wins.

➡ **Workbook p. 142, Activities 1 and 2**

Lesson 2 Student's Book p. 71

✔ **Homework Check!**
Workbook p. 142, Activities 1 and 2
Answers
1 Match the phrases.
1. c, 2. e, 3. f, 4. b, 5. a
2 Complete the e-mail with the words in box.
1. arrive, 2. check in, 3. print out, 4. go through,
5. board, 6. takes off, 7. lands, 8. pick up,
9. go through

Warm-up

Students play a game of *Hangman* to prepare for the lesson.
- Draw a hangman's noose similar to this one on the board:

- Choose one of the landmarks, for example, *the Statue of Liberty*. Write as many blanks as there are letters in the phrase, with slashes separating words:
  _ _ _ _ _ _ / _ _ / _ _ _ _ _ _ _
- Students form three or four teams. Each team calls out a letter. If the letter is in the word, fill it in. If it is not, write that letter to the side of the noose and begin to draw the man on the noose starting with his head.
- The next team calls out a letter and so on. Play until one of the team says the word or phrase or the man is "hung."
- You may have students come to the board to "play teacher" and choose the landmarks.

4 🎧²⁴ **Complete the messages with the words in the box. Then listen and check.**
Students complete sentences with human-made wonders vocabulary. They listen to the audio to check their answers.
Answers

1. temple, 2. statues, 3. stadium, 4. Pyramid,
5. Wall, 6. Mosque, 7. ruins, 8. bridge

Audio Script
1. This building is a temple at Angkor Wat in Cambodia. It's awesome!
2. Rapa Nui's mysterious *moai* statues stand on Easter Island.
3. I'm at the Colosseum in Rome. It's an ancient sports stadium where people watched races and fights.
4. This is the great pyramid of Giza in Egypt. It was once the tallest structure on Earth!
5. This is the Great Wall of China. It's a dream to be here!
6. The Blue Mosque in Turkey is one of the most important buildings in Islam.
7. These are the ruins of the ancient city of Machu Picchu in Peru. What a place!
8. The Ponte Vecchio is the most beautiful bridge in Florence, Italy. What a way to cross a river!

5 In your notebook, make a list of places like the ones in Activity 4 that are in your country. Are they easy to visit?
Students brainstorm places tourists like to visit in their own country and note whether the places are easy to visit.
Answers

Answers will vary.

6 Think Fast! In your notebook, write down as many types of building as you can, e.g., supermarket.
Students do a three-minute timed challenge: they list types of buildings or places in a city or town.
Answers

Answers will vary.

7 Imagine you traveled by plane to one of the places in Activity 4. Write a post for your friends at home. Include the information below.
In a creative personalization activity, students use air travel vocabulary to write about an imagined travel experience. Explain a punch line is an exciting or fun ending of their post. Ask them to circle the punchlines in Activity 4.
Answers

Answers will vary.

Extension
Students research one of the places from the lesson.
- Draw students' attention to the photos on page 71.
- Have students choose, or assign, one of the places to research.
- Have students present their findings to the class.
- Encourage them to use visual aids or to include some cultural component, such as music or food, with their presentation.

Wrap-up
Students practice vocabulary with a game of Pictionary.
- Students form groups of three or four.
- Set a stopwatch for two minutes.
- Students take turns drawing the landmarks from Activity 4 while the other students try to guess.
- The group that has successfully drawn and guessed the most landmarks when the stopwatch has gone off wins.

▶ **Workbook p. 143, Activities 3 and 4**

 Grammar

Objectives
Students will be able to express their travel **preferences** and to use **intensifiers**.

Lesson 3 Student's Book pp. 72 and 73

✔ **Homework Check!**
Workbook p. 143, Activities 3 and 4

Answers
3 Write the names of the countries under the correct landmarks.
1. Mexico, 2. Croatia, 3. Brazil, 4. US, 5. Italy, 6. Mexico, 7. Spain

4 Write the landmarks in Activity 3 in the correct columns.
Walls: Walls of Ston; *Statues:* Christ the Redeemer, David; *Pyramids:* Chichén Itzá; *Bridges:* Golden Gate, *Stadiums* Camp Nou; *Ruins:* Palenque

Warm-up
Students make an acrostic to generate interest and activate prior knowledge.
- Write the word TRAVEL vertically down the board.
- Students write words or phrases that tell about their experiences and attitudes about travel.
- Monitor, offering help as needed.
- Students form pairs and discuss what the words and phrases mean.

1 Answer the quiz and check your answers. Then compare with a partner.
Students are exposed to the target structures for expressing preferences as they answer the quiz to know how adventurous they are when they travel.

Answers
Answers will vary.

2 Circle the correct options to complete the sentences.
Draw students' attention to the *Preferences* box about preferences. Have them identify the three structures and explain that *I'd rather* is not followed by *to*. Then ask them to complete the sentences.

Answers
1. not, 2. to share, 3. wouldn't like to, 4. have, 5. to go

3 Complete the sentences so they are true for you. Then compare with a partner.
In a personalization activity, students complete the sentences with their own preferences.

Answers
Answers will vary.

Extension
Students play a game of Vacation Bingo.
- Prepare a set of cards with vacation activities from the unit and others your students know.
- Write these on the board.
- Have students make Bingo cards with up to 25 squares, with the center a FREE space.
- Students write the activities randomly on their cards.
- Put the set of cards in a bag or box. Draw one out at a time and say it aloud. If a student has that activity, she should put an X on the word.
- Continue drawing and saying activities.
- When a student has five Xs horizontally, diagonally or vertically, she shouts *Bingo!*
- The student should read the activities back to you to check that they have been called.
- Students can make other cards to continue the play.

Wrap-up
Students play a game of Two Truths and a Lie to consolidate the lesson.
- Draw students' attention to the statements in Activity 3.
- Students form pairs and take turns saying three of the statements; two are true and one is a lie. Students try to guess which is the lie.
- Monitor, offering help as needed. Encourage students to use the affirmative, negative and question forms of the target language.
- Come together as a class and have some students share what they learned about their classmates.

 Workbook p. 143, Activity 1

Lesson 4   Student's Book p. 73

> ✔ **Homework Check!**
> Workbook p. 143, Activitiy 1
> **Answers**
> **1 Circle the correct options to complete the sentences.**
> 1. I'd prefer, 2. I would like, 3. I'd prefer, 4. I'd rather, 5. wouldn't like

Warm-up

Students build a sentence chain to generate interest and activate prior knowledge.

- Draw a suitcase on the board. Say *We're going on vacation. What are you bringing?* Begin the sentence chain by saying something like *I'm bringing a pair of sunglasses.*

- A student then says what you're bringing and what he's / she's bringing, for example, [Your name] *is bringing a pair of sunglasses and I'm bringing sunscreen.*

- The next student then says what others before him are bringing: [Your name] *is bringing a pair of sunglasses, she's bringing sunscreen and I'm bringing a guidebook.*

- Continue with other students. If a student makes a mistake, he / she is out of the game.

4 🎧²⁵ **Listen to the conversation. Circle T (True) or F (False).**

Students are exposed to the use of *too* and *enough* as they listen and answer comprehension questions.

Answers
1. T, 2. F (Chase packed his suitcase.), 3. T, 4. F (Chase is nervous.)

Audio Script

MOM: Come on, Chase! You're too slow! Our taxi leaves in five minutes. What a start to the vacation!
CHASE: I'm sorry, Mom. It's just it's the first time that I've gone on vacation and I don't know what to pack in my suitcase.
MOM: Is it ready now?
CHASE: Yeah, here it is.
MOM: Did you pack it yourself?
CHASE: Yes!
MOM: Oh! These bags are too heavy. I'm not strong enough to pick this suitcase up.
CHASE: Really?
MOM: What did you put in here? Look at all these clothes! You don't need all these. You only need enough clothes for a three-day trip—not everything in your closet!
CHASE: I don't know. I'd rather take everything in case I need it.
MOM: You're too nervous. This is silly. Take something out of your bag!
CHASE: What if I need it later?
MOM: Oh! Chase!

5 🎧²⁵ **Listen again and complete the sentences in the box.**

Students read the information in the *Too and Enough* box and complete the example sentences.

Answers
1. heavy, 2. strong

6 Unscramble the sentences.

Students unscramble the words to practice word order when forming sentences using *too* and *enough*.

Answers
1. I don't have enough money for a new bike.
2. Spanish pronunciation is too difficult for me.
3. I have enough time today to go to the mall.
4. I'm old enough to see any movie at the theater.
5. My journey to school is too long.

7 In your notebook, change the sentences in Activity 6 so they are true for you.

Students write new sentences with their own information using the sentences in Activity 6.

Answers
Answers will vary.

Wrap-up

Students practice *too* and *enough* by debating controversial statements.

- Write some controversial statements on the board, for example: 1. *Football players are too wealthy.* 2. *Teachers don't make enough money.* 3. *Women are not strong enough to be effective leaders.* 4. *Students are given too much homework.*

- Students form groups of three or four and discuss their reactions to the statements.

- Monitor, offering help as needed. Encourage students to defend their positions using *too* and *(not) enough*.

➡ **Workbook p. 144, Activities 2 and 3**

Listening & Writing

Objectives
Students will be able to infer relationships between events and use past forms to write a narrative.

Lesson 5 Student's Book pp. 74 and 75

✔ **Homework Check!**
Workbook p. 144, Activities 2 and 3

Answers
2 Complete the sentences with *too* and *enough*.
1. too, 2. enough, 3. too, 4. enough, 5. too
3 Rewrite the sentences exchanging *too* for *enough* and vice versa. The sentences should have the same meaning.
1. She's too young. 2. It's not big enough. 3. The tea is not cool enough to drink. 4. He's too weak. 5. Is it too early to call?

Warm-up
Students preview a listening by creating a story.
- Draw students' attention to the illustrations in Activity 1.
- Students form groups of three. They decide on the order of the pictures and come up with a story using them.
- Monitor, offering help as needed.
- Have groups share their stories.
- Tell students they will listen and find out the actual story.

1 🎧²⁶ **Listen and number the pictures.**
Students listen to a story and number the illustrations in the order they hear them.

Answers
left to right 4, 5, 1, 2, 3

Audio Script
Last summer, my friend Chelsea had gone on vacation with her parents on a cruise through the Pacific. On the fourth night, she couldn't sleep and she decided to go for a walk.
On the main deck, she didn't see a lot of people. There was a man admiring the stars with a telescope. There was a couple standing near the flag pole. They were kissing. Chelsea blushed, turned around and began walking to the other side of the main deck.
Suddenly, she saw someone, or at least a shadow, jumping into the ocean. She screamed and immediately a crewman arrived and asked her if she was OK. "Someone has just jumped off the board, hurry, he might be still alive!" said Chelsea. The crewman asked her if she was sure about that.

"Yes! Well, I saw a shadow." The crewman reported the incident to the captain. Some crewmen looked for any evidence that indicated that someone had abandoned the ship, but they found nothing. Not knowing what else to do, Chelsea went back to her cabin and fell asleep.
The next morning, Chelsea woke up and wondered if everything had been a bad dream. She got up and went to look for her parents to have breakfast. On her way to the dining room she saw the captain talking to some crewmen. They looked very concerned. Chelsea felt a chill all over her body…

2 🎧²⁶ **Complete the story with the correct words. Then listen again to check.**
Students try to guess or recall the verbs that complete the story. They listen to the story again to check their answers.

Answers
1. gone, 2. standing, 3. has, 4. abandoned, 5. had, 6. felt

3 Read the story in Activity 2 again. Find two examples of each tense.
Students reread the story to identify examples of three narrative verb tenses.

Example Answers
1. decided, didn't see, 2. was… admiring, were kissing, 3. had gone, had abandoned

Stop and Think! Critical Thinking
Many people say "it was all a dream" is a bad ending to a story. Do you agree? Why? Why not?
- Ask *Do you think that ending a story with "it was all a dream" is a bad ending?*
- Students form pairs and explain their reasons.

Wrap-up
Students use illustrations to retell a story.
- Draw students' attention to the illustrations in Activity 1.
- Students form pairs and take turns retelling the story from the listening.
- Monitor, offering help as needed.
- Ask students to take turns retelling a bit of the story each around the room.

➡ **Workbook p. 145, Activities 1 and 2**

Lesson 6 — Student's Book p. 75

✔ **Homework Check!**
Workbook p. 145, Activities 1 and 2

Answers
1 Match each wall with its location. Then read and check your answers.
1. e, 2. a, 3. b, 4. d
2 Read the text again and circle *T* (True) or *F* (False).
1. T, 2. F (The Berlin Wall separated East and West Germany.), 3. F (The Wall of Troy is the subject of Homer's poem *The Iliad*.), 4. T

Warm-up
Students review verbs with a game of *Verb Charades* to prepare for their writing.
- Agree on some silent cues, for example: when you point behind you, the verb is in past tense; when you point to the ground, it's in present continuous; when you point ahead of you, it's in future. You may also wish to hold up fingers and tap them to your forearm to indicate the number of syllables in the verb.
- Start acting out a verb, indicating which tense. Review all three tenses with the cues.
- Students form groups of five or six and take turns acting out and guessing verbs.

4 In pairs, read the definition of Flash Fiction. In your notebooks, write the setting, characters and plot of the story in Activity 2. Discuss the ending of the story.
After learning about flash fiction, students work in pairs to write the elements of the story in Activity 2. The story has an open ending. Students discuss how they think the story ends.

Answers
Setting: cruise; *Characters*: Chelsea, the crewmen, the captain; *Plot*: a shadow fell off the deck

5 Work in small groups. In your notebook, write your piece of Flash Fiction (150 words). Read the guidelines below.
Using the story in Activity 2 as a model and following the guidelines given, students work in small groups to write a piece of flash fiction.
- Draw students' attention to the **Be Strategic!** box and read the information aloud.
- Encourage students to use different tenses while they write their piece of Flash Fiction.
- Monitor and provide help as needed.

6 Exchange your story with other groups. Which story was the most interesting? Why?
Groups read each other's stories and discuss what makes the stories interesting.

Extension
Students produce a play based on their Flash Fiction.
- Students form groups of three and choose one of their pieces of Flash Fiction.
- Guide students by having them identify the characters, setting and plot.
- Students work to write dialogue and stage directions, producing a play based on their Flash Fiction.
- Students perform their plays for the class.

Wrap-up
Students put stories in order to consolidate the lesson.
- Have students bring a copy of their stories to class.
- Students cut or tear their stories into sections.
- Students form pairs.
- Students try to put their partner's story in order.
- Monitor, offering help as needed.
- Students check to see if their partners ordered their stories correctly.

➡ **Workbook p. 145, Activity 3**

Preparing for the Next Lesson
Ask students to watch a video about Trains in Europe: goo.gl/tF8awn or invite them to look around on the website about types of trains in Europe: goo.gl/0FmrQg.

 Culture

Objectives
Students will be able to identify different types of trains and countries in Europe as well as use **human-made wonders** vocabulary.

Lesson 7 Student's Book pp. 76 and 77

> ✔ **Homework Check!**
> Workbook p. 145, Activity 3
> **Answers**
> 3 Look at the map on pages 76 and 77. Imagine you are taking an Interrail trip through Europe. In your notebook, describe your trip and include the following information.

Warm-up
Students make a KWL Chart to preview the topic.
- Draw a KWL Chart on the board, similar to following:

What I Know	What I Want to Know	What I Have Learned

- Ask students to think about what they know about traveling by train in Europe and what they want to know.
- Tell students that they will read about traveling by train in Europe.

1 Read about a way to travel through Europe.
Students read the text about traveling by train through Europe and some of the types of trains there are.
- Ask students to read about interrailing in Europe.
- Draw students' attention to the **Guess What!** box. Tell them that before the euro appeared in 2002, every country in Europe had a different currency. Germany used marks, France used francs, Italy used lira, etc.

2 Read the clues and solve the crossword.
Using the clues and the text, students solve the crossword puzzle.

Answers
1. modern, 2. fast, 3. expensive, 4. budget, 5. scenery, 6. sleep, 7. connect, 8. ferry, 9. high-speed

Wrap-up
Students complete their KWL Charts.
- Students take out their KWL Charts from the Warm-up and complete the final column.
- Students form small groups of three or four and share what they have learned.
- Encourage students to discuss some of the following questions:
  » *What was the most interesting thing you learned?*
  » *What was the most surprising thing you learned?*
  » *Have you ever traveled by train? If so, share your experiences.*
  » *Would you like to travel by train through Europe? Why or why not?*
- Monitor, offering help as needed.
- Come together as a class and have some students share their thoughts and ideas.

 (No homework today.)

Teaching Tip
Providing Guided Practice
The more we work on a new skill, the better we get at it. Especially important is the guidance we receive from an expert. This is also true for education and learning. Guided practice, which follows direct instruction, can take a few shapes:
- Whole class. After teaching a new concept, support your students by giving them a highly controlled activity, such as a gap fill or multiple choice exercise. During this time, you are walking around the room, monitoring students and making sure they are on track. Then, to confirm understanding, you choose a few students to write their answers on the board; after which, the class checks the answers.
- Small group. Guided learning groups can be effective when students are struggling with particular skills or concepts. Keep in mind students' levels and personalities (shy vs. outgoing), when grouping students for practice. More proficient students can support others when they need it.
- Individual. When appropriate, you can meet with individual students and teach one-on-one. If you notice a student struggling during whole class or small group practice, make sure to spend time with the student when you set up any independent practice. This way you can correct misunderstandings of concepts before students are expected to apply skills without help.

Lesson 8   Student's Book pp. 76 and 77

Warm-up
Students play a game of Scattergories to activate prior knowledge and generate interest.
- Write categories horizontally on the board that relate to the unit.
- Students form groups of four or five. One group member is the secretary; he writes down the categories as headers on a piece of paper.
- Ask students to say a letter of the alphabet.
- Tell students that they need to try to think of at least one word for each category that begins with the letter circled.
- Set a stopwatch for two to three minutes. When the stopwatch goes off, have students read aloud their words.
- The group with most words either wins or gets a point, if you wish to continue playing with another letter.

3 🎧²⁷ **Listen to two friends preparing for their Interrail trip. Mark (✓) the places they mention.**
Students listen to the conversation and mark the places the speakers mention.

Answers
A bridge, A museum, A stadium, A temple, A wall, Ruins

Audio Script
MIKE: I cannot believe we're going to go to Europe, Emily!
EMILY: I know, Mike. It's like a dream!
MIKE: OK, let's look at our route.
EMILY: We start in London, England. We'll take a photo of Tower Bridge, won't we?
MIKE: Of course we will!
EMILY: Then we go to Harwich. At Harwich, we take a ferry to Rotterdam.
MIKE: Uh-huh.
EMILY: Then we go from Rotterdam to Amsterdam.
MIKE: What do we do in Amsterdam?
EMILY: We visit the Van Gogh Museum.
MIKE: Cool. After Amsterdam?
EMILY: We get a train to Germany and we go to Berlin.
MIKE: In Berlin we can see the Berlin Wall.
EMILY: That's right.
MIKE: So after Berlin, we go to Paris.
EMILY: Yes, and in Paris we see the Eiffel Tower, the Louvre with its famous glass pyramids and other things.
MIKE: All this art! I like sports, you know.
EMILY: Don't worry. After Paris, we go to Barcelona in Spain. You can visit the Nou Camp stadium there…
MIKE: The home of Barcelona! Awesome!
EMILY: Then we cheat a little…
MIKE: Why?
EMILY: From Barcelona we get a plane!
MIKE: Where to?
EMILY: To Athens in Greece where we see the ruins. There's a famous temple there.
MIKE: Amazing. Europe is so cool.

4 🎧²⁷ **Listen again. Trace their route on the map.**
Students listen again for detailed information and trace the speakers' planned route on the map.

Answers
London, Harwich, Rotterdam, Amsterdam, Berlin, Paris, Barcelona, Athens

5 Think Fast! Name the ten countries where the cities on the map are located.
Students do a two-minute timed challenge: they name the country for each city on the map.

Answers
Dublin, Ireland, *London*, England / UK, *Harwich*, England / UK, *Lisbon*, Portugal, *Madrid*, Spain, *Barcelona*, Spain, *Paris*, France, *Brussels*, Belgium, *Rotterdam*, the Netherlands, *Amsterdam*, the Netherlands, *Berlin*, Germany, *Munich*, Germany, *Milan*, Italy, *Rome*, Italy, *Thessaloniki*, Greece, *Athens*, Greece

Wrap-up
Students discuss preferences to consolidate the lesson.
- Students form pairs. Tell students they are traveling companions. They are traveling for one week and will go to four cities.
- Students work in pairs to decide on their trips.
- Monitor, offering help as needed.
- Come together as a class and have students share their trips. Encourage them say why they chose the places they did.

▶ **(No homework today.)**

Objectives
Students will be able to express their preferences and use **air travel** vocabulary to write a travel guide.

Lesson 9 — Student's Book pp. 78 and 79

Warm-up
Students play a game of *Two Truths and a Lie* to generate interest and prepare for the lesson.
- Tell students about three places you've visited. Two are actual places you've been to, but one is a lie. Give them details such as when you were there, where you stayed, what you did there and your impression of the place.
- Tell students to think of three places, two they've actually visited and one that they will lie about.
- Students form small groups of three or four and share their places. They ask and answer questions to determine which one is the lie.
- Monitor, offering help as needed.

1 Think Fast! Make a list of the most common places of tourist accommodation.
Students do a one-minute timed challenge: they list the types of places tourists stay in.

Answers
Answers will vary.

2 Choose a destination you would like to visit. Mark (✓) the information you need to know before your trip.
Students think of a destination and categorize information about the destination in the table according to how important it is to know before visiting.

Answers
Answers will vary.

3 Number the texts with the questions in Activity 2.
Students read the travel information texts and identify which question in Activity 2 is answered in each paragraph.

Answers
a. 4, b. 3, c. 2, d. 1, e. 5, f. 4

4 Discuss the reasons why you would prefer or would rather not go to the resort in Activity 3 with a partner.
Pairs discuss the resort described in Activity 3 using language to express preferences.

Wrap-up
Students survey each other to consolidate for the lesson.
- Draw students' attention to the map on page 77.
  Ask *Has anyone visited any of these places?*
  Elicit responses.
- If you have a world map, display that.
- Say *Think about the places you've visited. Make a list.*
- Have students form groups of three or four. Students tell the others about the places they've been. One student acts as secretary and makes a list.
- Come together as a class and have each group share the places their group members have visited.
- Monitor, offering help as needed.
- Note which places are the most popular, most unusual, furthest away and closest.

 Teaching Tip

Using Less-Controlled and Freer Activities
Controlled and freer practice can be thought of on a spectrum, where you choose the level of control for tasks, based on the needs of your students and the progression of the lesson. Here are some guidelines for using less-controlled and freer activities:
- Less-controlled activities are effective as confidence and familiarity in the language increases. In these activities, there is a somewhat increased amount of freedom, which can also increase the challenge and interest. You cannot guess all the specific answers before the activity begins, although there are a limited number of possibilities. For example, if students were to brainstorm famous landmarks, you can anticipate which landmarks your students will know, but there will be a few that are unanticipated and surprising. Less-controlled activities give students the opportunity to somewhat personalize the language, drawing on prior knowledge.
- Finally, freer activities come last in the lesson. Here students have complete freedom in the language they produce. You cannot predict what will be said before the activity begins, although effectively timed freer activities have prepped students to use the target structures. This real, relevant practice naturally leads to high rates of retention. This can take the form of a discussion, a role play or a writing assignment in essay or poem form.

Lesson 10 Student's Book p. 79

Warm-up

Students play a guessing game to prepare for the lesson.
- Think of a destination you've been to and how you would answer the questions in Activity 2.
- Draw students' attention to the chart in Activity 2.
- Tell students that you are thinking of a destination. They ask questions, including the ones in Activity 2, in order to guess.
- Say *Think about the destination you chose. Keep it a secret.*
- Students form groups of four or five. They take turns asking and answering questions, trying to guess each other's destination.
- Monitor, offering help as needed.

5 **Think of the destination you chose in Activity 2. In small groups, write a guide for travelers like the one in Activity 3. Use the Internet to research your ideas.**
Using the prompts listed, students research the destination they chose for Activity 2 and write a guide for the destination, using the example in Activity 3 as a model. Encourage students to be creative and choose a destination with many attractions.

6 **Exchange your guide with another group. Imagine you're spending one day together in the place suggested. Discuss and agree on what to do that day.**
Groups exchange their guides and discuss each other's destinations, expressing their preferences of activities to do in the place.

The Digital Touch
To incorporate digital media in the project, suggest one or more of the following:
- Watch this video for tips on making a tour guide: goo.gl/5KgBh5.

Note that students should have the option to do a task on paper or digitally.

Extension
Students make a travel mind map.
- Draw a circle on the board. Write *travel* in the center.
- Students form pairs and use the information from the unit to make a mind map with all the travel expressions and vocabulary, topics, places and landmarks, etc., which they've learned.

Wrap-up

Students take a poll on the most popular destinations.
- Draw students' attention to their own guides.
- Display them around the room. Post a piece of paper under each one.
- Tell students to look at the guides and decide which place they'd most like to go to.
- Students read the guides and "sign up" to go on one trip each.
- When students have finished, discuss which trips were the most popular and have students share why they made their choices.

➡ **Workbook p. 144, Activity 1 (Review)**

Review

Objectives
Students will be able to consolidate their understanding of the **air travel** and **human-made wonders** vocabulary as well as preferences and intensifiers.

Lesson 11   Student's Book p. 80

> ✔ **Homework Check!**
> Workbook p. 144, Activity 1 (Review)
> **Answers**
> **1 Mark the sentences correct (✓) or incorrect (✗). Rewrite the incorrect sentences.**
> 1. ✗ She'd prefer <u>to</u> learn Spanish, but she doesn't have enough time. 2. ✓, 3. ✗ He doesn't have <u>enough</u> experience to get the job. 4. ✓, 5. ✗ I'd prefer not <u>to</u> go to the ruins because it's raining.

Warm-up
Students play a game of *Taboo* to review vocabulary.
- Students form groups of five or six.
- Place chairs, one for each group, in front of the class, with the backs to the board. Spread the chairs out as far as possible.
- Groups choose one person to sit in the "hot seat" at the front of the class.
- Write one of the vocabulary items from page 70 on the board. Explain that groups should try to explain the word to their group's student in the hot seat. They may not use any forms of the word or words on the board.
- Once a group's student has said the word, award them a point.
- Groups choose another student to sit in the hot seat.
- Write another word on the board and continue the game until you have reviewed all the vocabulary.

1 Follow and write the words for air travel.
Students follow the lines connecting each box to a photo and write the corresponding vocabulary words or phrases.
Answers
top to bottom boarding pass, customs, passport, airport, visa stamps, luggage / suitcases

2 Circle the correct options to complete the sentences.
Students identify the words that correctly complete each collocation related to air travel.
Answers
1. boarding, 2. pick up, 3. takes off, 4. check in, 5. take off, 6. book, 7. go through, 8. print them out

3 Look at the icons and write the places. What is the mystery word?
Students identify places vocabulary words and use them to complete a crossword puzzle.
Answers
1. mosque, 2. statue, 3. wall, 4. bridge, 5. pyramid, 6. ruins, 7. temple; *mystery word* stadium

Extension
Students play a game of *Memory* to review places and landmarks.
- Have students count off by As and Bs.
- Have students take out a piece of paper. Students cut or tear it into eight pieces. Draw students' attention to Activity 4 on page 71. Student A should write the names of the landmarks. Student B should write the places where the landmarks are.
- Students form pairs, A and B, and shuffle their cards together. They place them face-down between them.
- Student A turns over two cards. If they match, that is, are the landmark and its corresponding location, she keeps it. If not, she turns the cards over, keeping them in the same place, and Student B turns two cards over.
- Students play until all cards have been matched. The student with the most cards wins.

Wrap-up
Students play a game of *Last One Standing* to review vocabulary.
- Say a vocabulary topic, for example, *landmarks*.
- Clap out a beat and say *One, two, three …* and say a topic-related word, for example, *the Leaning Tower of Pisa*.
- Clap out the beat again and say *One, two, three … * and call on a student to say a word or phrase related to the topic.
- Continue until a student can't think of a word or repeats one that's been said. That student sits down.
- Continue, saying new topics as vocabulary is exhausted, for example, *things you need to travel by plane, stages of traveling by plane, structures and buildings you see when you travel, trains in Europe, cities / countries in Europe*.
- The winner is the last one standing.

▶ **(No homework today.)**

Lesson 12   Student's Book p. 81

Warm-up

Students review grammar with a football game.

- Draw the following football field on the board:

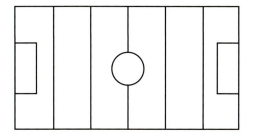

- Divide the class into two teams. Draw a symbol for Team A at one end of the field and another symbol for Team B.
- Flip a coin to see which team will be Team A and go first.
- Ask a student from Team A a grammar item (see below).
- If the student is correct, move his marker one space up the field. If not, a student from Team B gets a chance to answer it.
- Continue playing. When a team's marker gets to the last line before the goal, ask a question. If the student answers the question correctly, she "scores a goal."
- Play until you have covered all you want to review. The team with the most goals wins.
- Here are some items you can use in your review:
  » *Complete the sentence: He's ___ old to play games.* (too)
  » *Complete the sentence: Are you well ___ to go to school?* (enough)
  » *Complete the sentence: I prefer swimming. It's ___ hot to go hiking.* (too)
  » *Complete the sentence: I'm hungry ___ to eat anything!* (enough)
  » *Respond with your own information: Do you want to go to Athens or Rome?*
  » *Respond with your own information: Which do you like better—skiing or snowboarding?*
  » *Respond with your own information: What would you like to do this afternoon?*
  » *Respond with your own information: Do you like traveling by train or plane?*
  » *Respond with your own information: Do you want to go to Athens or Rome?*

4 Complete the posts with the words in the boxes. There's one extra in each post.

Students complete the sentences with the human-made wonders vocabulary.

Answers

1. pyramids, 2. wall, 3. stadium, 4. bridge, 5. statue, 6. ruins

5 Complete the conversations with the correct form of the verbs in parentheses.

Students choose the correct form of each verb to complete the expressions of preferences.

Answers

1. to go, 2. wash, 3. to play, 4. to wear, 5. to sleep

6 Complete the sentences with *too* or *enough*.

Students determine whether *too* or *enough* correctly completes each sentence.

Answers

1. too, 2. enough, 3. enough, 4. too, 5. enough

❓ Big Question

Students are given the opportunity to revisit the Big Question and reflect on it.

- Ask students to turn to the unit opener on page 69 and think about the question *Where would you rather go?*
- Ask students to think about the discussions they've had on travel, the readings they've read, the texts they've listened to and the tour guide they made.
- Students form small groups to discuss the following:
  » *Do you like to travel? Why or why not?*
  » *What's more important for you when you travel, comfort or price?*
  » *Do you prefer to have a more adventurous or relaxing vacation?*
  » *Do you prefer to go back to the same place on vacation or travel to different places?*
  » *Do you think that traveling changes a person? Explain.*
- Monitor, offering help as needed, particularly with vocabulary.

⭐ Scorecard

Hand out (and/or project) a *Scorecard*. Have students fill in their *Scorecards* for this unit.

➡ **Study for the unit test.**

6 Why do we behave the way we do?

Grammar
Modal Verbs (+,-): Ashley <u>could</u> use her sister's ID card to go to the disco. She was nervous because the bouncer <u>may</u> look at her card. Sienna <u>might</u> think Ashley took the wrong card by mistake.

Vocabulary
Phrasal Verbs: break up, figure out, get along, get over, give up, go on, keep it to yourself, turn in, own up, tell on someone

Reading
Reading moral dilemmas

Writing
Using transition words for contradiction to write a solution to a moral dilemma

Why do we behave the way we do?

In the first lesson, read the unit title aloud and have students look carefully at the unit cover. Encourage them to think about the message in the picture. At the end of the unit, students will discuss the big question: *Why do we behave the way we do?*

Teaching Tip
Providing an Effective Model
Students will have a stronger belief that they can accomplish the goal if they follow steps that were demonstrated effectively for them.
- Actually do the activity, or part of it, pointing out every transitional step.
- Share your thinking process aloud and give examples.
- Have students follow along when appropriate.
- Utilize other students to help, particularly with a role play.
- When possible, give students a chance to practice the activity before they perform the task.

Vocabulary

Objective
Students will be able to use **phrasal verbs** to talk about moral dilemmas.

Lesson 1 — Student's Book p. 84

Warm-up
Students brainstorm ideas to generate interest and activate prior knowledge.
- Students form groups of three or four.
- Draw students' attention to the pictures of the unit opener on page 83.
- Ask *Why do you think people are behaving as they are? What are the situations?*
- Groups discuss what they think is happening in each picture.
- Monitor, offering help as needed.
- Have students compare their ideas with other groups.

1 Read the definitions of *dilemma*. Then look at the words below and cross out the ones that are not mentioned.
Students read the definitions and cross out the words in the list that are not related to the definitions of *dilemma*.

Answers

~~consensus, agreement~~

2 Choose the best definition for you. Compare with a partner.
Students choose the definition of dilemma they like best and discuss their choice with a partner.

Answers

Answers will vary.

3 Read the dilemmas. Rank them from 1 (least difficult) to 6 (most difficult) in the boxes. Don't share your answers yet.
Working individually, students read and analyze the dilemmas to rank them in order of controversy.

Answers

Answers will vary.

Stop and Think! Value
How do values affect the way we solve dilemmas?
- Draw a mind map in the form of a web on the board. Write *Values* in the center circle.
- Elicit some things that affect our values, for example, *family, friends, culture, income level.*
- Students form pairs or small groups and complete their own mind map.
- Ask *How do values affect the way we solve dilemmas?*
- Students discuss in pairs or small groups.

- Monitor, offering help as needed.
- Come together as a class having some students share their thoughts and ideas.

Extension
Students play a game of *Taboo* to review phrasal verbs.
- Divide the class into two or three groups. Set a chair in front of each group so that the backs are to the board.
- Write one of the phrasal verbs on the board.
- Each team tries to describe the phrasal verb to the student in the "hot seat," without using the phrasal verb or any forms of it.
- Once a student has guessed the phrasal verb, erase.
- The student that describes the word successfully gets a point for his / her group.
- Erase the phrasal verb, have new students sit in the hot seat and write another phrasal verb on the board.
- Continue until you have reviewed all the phrasal verbs from the unit.
- The team with the most points wins.

Wrap-up
Students play a game of *Memory* to review phrasal verbs.
- Students take out a piece of paper and cut or tear it into ten pieces.
- They count off A and B.
- Draw students' attention to the highlighted blue phrasal verbs in the text in Activity 3.
- Student A writes the verb part of each phrasal verb; student B writes the preposition part of each.
- Students form pairs, Student A and Student B.
- They combine their cards and spread them out face-down between them.
- Students take turns turning over two cards. If the cards match and make both parts of a phrasal verb, the student keeps the pair and turns over two more. If the cards don't match, play goes to the other student.
- Students play until all phrasal verbs are matched. The student with the most cards wins.
- Ask them to keep the cards for the Review in Lesson 11.

➡ **Workbook p. 146, Activities 1 and 2**

Lesson 2 Student's Book p. 85

✔ **Homework Check!**
Workbook p. 146, Activities 1 and 2
Answers
1 Match each phrasal verb to its meaning.
1. b, 2. c, 3. a, 4. f, 5. g, 6. e
2 Underline the sentence that describes each picture.
1. They just broke up. 2. He wants to own up to what he did. 3. He's keeping the gossip to himself. 4. My brother hasn't gotten over his ex-girlfriend. 5. I give up!

Warm-up

Students make sentence chains to review phrasal verbs.
- Begin by saying a sentence with the verb part of a phrasal verb, for example, *I can't always get…* Indicate that a student should finish the sentence, for example, *along with my brother.*
- That student begins another sentence with the verb part of a phrasal verb. Another student finishes the sentence.
- Continue until all phrasal verbs are reviewed.

4 Match the phrasal verbs in Activity 3 to their definitions.
Students determine the meaning of the phrasal verbs from context and match them to their definitions.

Answers

1. f, 2. i, 3. j, 4. c, 5. g, 6. b, 7. h, 8. a, 9. e, 10. d

5 Now, in small groups, identify the dilemma you each ranked number 6. Discuss why it was the most difficult one for you.
Students go back over their own rankings in Activity 3 and explain in small groups why they found the one ranked number 6 most difficult.
- Tell students to have a brief debate on which dilemma was more controversial for them.
- Draw students' attention to the **Guess What!** box. Tell them that if you are facing a very difficult decision or you have two very unpleasant alternatives to choose from you say, "I'm between a rock and a hard place."

Answers

Answers will vary.

6 🎧²⁸ Circle the correct options to complete the sentences. Listen and check.
Students identify the phrasal verb that best completes each sentence and listen to the audio to check their answers.

Answers

1. get, 2. out, 3. tell, 4. kept, 5. up, 6. own, 7. turned, 8. over, 9. up, 10. on

Audio Script

1. Hannah's having problems in her French class because she doesn't get along with her teacher.
2. I cannot figure out what's wrong with my science homework.
3. I know I didn't go to basketball practice, but please don't tell on me.
4. I told Paula my secret and thankfully she kept it to herself.
5. Keep practicing the song—don't give up. You'll get it right soon.
6. I had to own up to stealing the pen. I felt bad about it.
7. That movie was amazing! I can't believe the murderer's mother turned him in to the police.
8. Simon never got over his parents' divorce.
9. Thalia isn't happy because she just broke up with her boyfriend.
10. The teacher told the class to stop laughing at the new boy, but they went on doing it.

7 In pairs, take turns asking each other the questions.
Students practice using the phrasal verbs in a speaking activity, asking and answering the questions.

Wrap-up

Play a game of *Casino* to review separable and inseparable phrasal verbs.
- Have them choose names for their teams and write the names, plus *$500* for each team, on the board.
- Say a sentence with one of the phrasal verbs, either correctly separated by an object or not.
- Students bet up to $100 on whether or not they think the sentence is correct.
- "Pay" students their winnings by adding to their $500 if correct. Deduct their losses from the $500 if incorrect.

The group with the most "money" wins.

▶ **Workbook p. 147, Activity 3**

> 💭 **Teaching Tip**
> **Limiting Dictionary Use**
> Try to limit the amount of time students spend consulting a dictionary. Asking students to memorize words and phrases is fine, but make sure that the majority of class time is spent putting these words and phrases into practice rather than just reciting words from a dictionary. This can become repetitive and boring, and provides little context to make your lesson relevant.

Grammar

Objective
Students will be able to use the **modal verbs** *might*, *could* and *may* for possibility.

Lesson 3 — Student's Book p. 86

> ✔ **Homework Check!**
> Workbook p. 147, Activity 3
> **Answers**
> **3 Mark (✓) the type of phrasal verb in each sentence. Rewrite the sentence if the phrasal verb is separable.**
> 1. inseparable, 2. separable, Lizzy figured the riddle out! 3. separable, She had to give running up after she broke her leg.

Warm-up
Students play a game testing their memories to generate interest.
- Draw students' attention to the illustrations in Activity 1.
- Students study the illustrations for one minute and then close their books.
- Students form pairs and take turns describing the illustrations.
- When students have finished, have them open their books to check their memories.

1 Look at the pictures and number them in the order they happened.
Students determine the narrative sequence of the illustrations and number each scene accordingly.
Answers
top row 2, 6, 3, *bottom row* 4, 5, 1

2 🎧29 Listen to a radio show and check your answers to Activity 1.
Students listen to the story that corresponds to the illustrations in Activity 1 and check their answers.

Audio Script
Now on the show, it's "moral dilemmas." Today's story is about two teenage sisters called Ashley and Sienna. Ashley is with her friends and they want to go to a disco. The disco is for over 18's only, but Ashley is only 15. She can't go to the disco because she is too young.
At home, Ashley is with her sister, Sienna. Sienna is 18. Sienna goes out and she leaves her ID card in her bag. Ashley could use her sister's ID card to go to the disco. The sisters look similar.
Ashley takes her sister's ID card. She leaves her own ID card at home. Sienna might think Ashley took the wrong card by mistake.
Later that evening, Ashley and her friends were outside the disco. She was nervous because the bouncer may look at her card. But she might not have any problems.
Unfortunately, the bouncer checked everybody's ID cards very carefully.
He picked up the phone. He could call her parents… or the police!
Ashley panics. They might send her to prison!
Finally, the police arrived and they took her home. Her parents were furious and Sienna was very angry that Ashley took her ID card.
That's today's moral dilemma. How bad was Ashley's crime? Would you do the same in her situation? What punishment could her parents give her? What may happen next?

3 🎧29 Listen again and complete the sentences.
Students complete the sentences with words from the audio.
Answers
1. disco, 2. Ashley, 3. mistake, 4. nervous, 5. problems, 6. parents, 7. panics

4 Look at the sentences in Activity 3 and answer the questions.
Students determine whether the events described in Activity 3 are possible, unlikely or not possible.
Answers
1. 2, 4, 5, 6; 2. 3, 7; 3. 1

> **Extension**
> Students play a game of *What's that Noise?* to practice modals of possibility.
> - Bring to class some everyday objects you can use to make noises.
> - Make a noise behind a screen so students can't see the objects.
> - Students make guesses about what the noises could be using modals.

Wrap-up
Students create original sentences about a listening to consolidate the lesson.
- Draw students' attention to the illustrations in Activity 1.
- Students form pairs and say as much as they can remember about the listening, using the illustrations as prompts.
- Monitor, offering help as needed.

➧ **Workbook p. 147, Activities 1 and 2**

Lesson 4   Student's Book p. 87

> ✔ **Homework Check!**
> Workbook p. 147, Activities 1 and 2
> **Answers**
> **1** In your notebook, write a sentence to describe each blurry picture. Use *might, could* or *may*.
> Answers will vary.
> **2** Read the dilemmas. Write the possible solutions with *might, could* or *may*. See the grammar box on page 87.
> Answers will vary.

Warm-up
Students try to solve a mystery to preview modals.
- Say *Sherlock Holmes is a famous fictional British detective. You are going to help him solve a murder mystery.*
- Then say the following facts:
  » *The famous racing horse, Silver Blaze, has been stolen.*
  » *The horse's trainer was found dead in the stables.*
  » *Next to the body, the dog who lives at the stables was standing.*
  » *Sherlock Holmes notes, "It's curious that the dog didn't bark."*
- Students form pairs to try to figure out the mystery.
- Take note of any usage of modals.
- Have some students share their ideas.
- Tell students solution to the mystery: *The owner of the dog stole the horse and killed the trainer. (The dog wouldn't bark at his owner.)*

5 **Read each prompt and color the degree of possibility in each chart. Then write sentences with *might, could* and *may*.**
Students decide how possible they think each event is and color the chart to reflect it. They write the sentences using the cues and the corresponding modal verbs.
- Draw students' attention to the ***might / could / may for possibility*** box and point out how we form sentences with modal verbs.
- Ask students to color the charts and write the sentences.

Answers
Answers will vary.

6 **In small groups, discuss the questions at the end of the radio show.**
Students discuss Ashley's dilemma and predict how the story ends.

7 **Think Fast!** **How many times have you been grounded? Why?**
Students do a three-minute timed challenge: they personalize the discussion.
- Draw students' attention to the **Guess What!** box. Tell them that the most common punishment for teenagers in the US is being grounded. When you're grounded, you're not allowed to go out with your friends and you have to stay home. "You're grounded, young lady!"

8 **In your notebook, complete the sentences with *might, could* or *may*. Then compare with a partner.**
Students complete the sentences with their own ideas and compare their answers in pairs. Encourage them to use the modal verbs.

Answers
Answers will vary.

Stop and Think! Critical Thinking
What is the legal age to consume alcoholic beverages in your country? Do you agree? Why or why not?
- Ask students to brainstorm different occasions when people drink.
- Elicit the legal drinking age in your students' country/ies.
- Ask *Do you agree with this policy? Why or why not?*
- Students form small groups to discuss.

> **Extension**
> Students speculate about objects to practice modals.
> - Have students bring in an object. The object should have some sort of story behind it, for example, how old it is, where it came from or what it's used for.
> - Students form groups of five or six and show each other their objects.
> - They take turns speculating about the objects.
> - After all students have speculated about each object, each student tells his classmates the story behind it.

Wrap-up
Students play a guessing game to practice modals.
- Model by showing your students a very expressive face, for example, look very angry or sad.
- Ask *What happened that made me feel this way?* Elicit some answers, encouraging students to use *might, could* and *may*.
- Students form groups of four or five and try to guess each other's feelings.

▶ **Workbook p. 148, Activity 3**

Reading & Writing

Objectives
Students will be able to read moral dilemmas and to use transition words for contradiction to write a solution to a moral dilemma.

Lesson 5 — Student's Book p. 88

✔ **Homework Check!**
Workbook p. 148, Activity 3

Possible answers
3 Rewrite the sentences using one of the words or phrases in the box above. More than one answer is possible.
1. Many people didn't want to leave their homes despite / in spite of the hurricane warnings. 2. Although / Even though I grew up in a poor neighborhood, I went to college and became a professor. 3. Ben and Amanda broke up although / even though they spent a lot of time together. 4. Despite / In spite of some bad grades, Jimena got into college.

Warm-up

 90

Students brainstorm moral dilemmas to activate prior knowledge and generate interest.
- Draw a mind map in the form of a web on the board. Write *moral dilemmas* in the center.
- Elicit some examples of moral dilemmas (parents, dating, money, friends) and write them in the map.
- Students form pairs and create their own mind map of moral dilemmas. They discuss possible scenarios for each.
- Monitor, offering help as needed.
- Have pairs share their ideas with another pair.

1 Work in groups of three. Each student reads one moral dilemma: A, B or C. Complete the table with information for your corresponding dilemma.
Students read a dilemma and summarize the problem and a solution in the table.
- Draw students' attention to the *Guess What!* box. Tell them that in most countries, the bills that people use for paper money get bigger as the value increases. In the US, all dollar bills are the same size. A $100 bill is the same size as a $1 bill!
- Ask them to what moral dilemma the *Guess What!* box refers to (Moral Dilemma C).

Answers
Answers will vary.

2 In your groups, follow the instructions.
Students discuss the dilemmas and possible solutions in small groups. They decide which dilemma is most difficult.

3 Read three possible solutions to moral dilemmas A, B and C. Write the correct number of each solution in Activity 1.
Students match the solutions to the dilemmas in Activity 1.

Answers
A. 2, B. 3, C. 1

Extension

Students write and respond to other moral dilemmas.
- Elicit some of the moral dilemmas from the Warm-up and pages 87 and 88.
- Students form groups of three or four and write five moral dilemmas.
- Monitor, offering help as needed.
- When students have finished, have them exchange their moral dilemmas with another group.
- Groups decide how they would respond to the moral dilemmas.
- Come together as a class and have groups share their responses.
- Encourage students to critique the responses.

Wrap-up

Students react to solutions to consolidate the lesson.
- Students meet with the groups they formed in Activity 1.
- Students discuss their reactions to the solution offered in Activity 3. Do they agree? Why or why not?
- Groups come up with another possible solution and present it to the class.

▶ **Workbook p. 149, Activities 1 and 2**

Lesson 6 Student's Book p. 89

✔ **Homework Check!**

Workbook p. 149, Activities 1 and 2

Answers

1 Read the article and write the numbers of the missing headings.
1. d, 2. c, 3. b, 4. a

2 Read the dilemma. In your notebook, write the number of tip(s) from the article you recommend and explain why.
Answers will vary.

Warm-up

Students make an acrostic to generate interest.
- Write the word *DILEMMA* vertically down the board.
- Students form pairs and write sentences giving advice for handling dilemmas that begin with those letters.
- Monitor, offering help as needed.
- Come together as a class and have some students share their acrostics.

4 Underline the phrases to express contrast in Activity 3.
Students reread the paragraphs in Activity 3 and identify the phrases that express contrast.
- Draw students' attention to the *Be Strategic!* box and read the information aloud.

Answers

1. In spite of the fact that, 2. Even though,
3. Despite, Although

5 Complete the sentences with words and phrases to express contrast. More than one answer is possible.
Using the phrases to express contrast from the *Be Strategic!* box, students complete the sentences.

Answers

1. Although / Even though / In spite of the fact that / Despite the fact that, 2. despite / in spite of, 3. even though / despite the fact that / in spite of the fact that, 4. Despite / In spite of, 5. despite / in spite of

6 Choose one of the dilemmas below. Then complete the table. In your notebook, write a paragraph with your solution.
Students summarize one of the dilemmas in the table and write a paragraph giving a solution.

Answers

Answers will vary.

Wrap-up

Students write their own moral dilemmas and solutions to consolidate the lesson.
- Draw students' attention to the moral dilemmas in Activity 6. Elicit examples of other moral dilemmas.
- Students form pairs and write an original moral dilemma.
- Pairs swap dilemmas.
- Each student writes a solution to their moral dilemma.
- Monitor, offering help as needed.
- When pairs have finished. Have them compare their solutions.
- Come together as a class and have some pairs share their solutions. Were they similar or very different?

 Workbook p. 149, Activity 3

Preparing for the Next Lesson
Ask students to read an introduction to South Korea: goo.gl/4LErfx or invite them to watch the video about a typical Korean's life goo.gl/WQsxIZ.

Teaching Tip

Giving Homework to Maximize English Exposure

Your students will most likely be going back to a household that does not regularly use English in conversation. This acts as an additional challenge for your students to overcome. While no student jumps at the chance to do more homework, giving your students work to practice on when they are away from the classroom is the best way to ensure that they aren't completely forgetting the English they learned in your class that day.

Culture

Objective
Students will be able to understand South Korean etiquette.

Lesson 7 Student's Book pp. 90 and 91

✔ **Homework Check!**
Workbook p. 149, Activity 3
Answers
3 Follow the instructions.
Answers will vary.

Warm-up
Students make a KWL Chart to preview the topic.
- Draw a KWL Chart on the board, similar to following:

What I Know	What I Want to Know	What I Have Learned

- Ask students to think about what they know about South Korea and what they want to know.
- Tell students that they will read about South Korea.

1 🎧30 **Circle the correct options to complete the fact file. Then listen and check.**
Students determine which facts correctly complete the file about South Korea and listen to check their answers.
Answers
1. Asia, 2. North, 3. Samsung, 4. Seoul, 5. 2012

Audio Script
The Korean peninsula is in East Asia. The peninsula is divided into two countries: democratic South Korea and communist North Korea. South Korea is one of the world's most technologically advanced countries. It is home to many famous technology companies like LG and Samsung. The capital, Seoul, was the host of the Olympic Games in 1988 and the soccer World Cup in 2002 along with Japan. This was the first World Cup to be hosted by two countries. The most famous person from South Korea is the pop star Psy, and you might know his song "Gangnam Style," which was a massive hit in 2012.

2 **Read Madison's blog. Then match the number of tips to the pictures.**
Students read the text and identify the photograph that corresponds to each tip.
Answers
top to bottom 4, 5, 3, 1, 2

Stop and Think! Critical Thinking
Why is it useful to know the customs of a place you have never been to?
- Ask your students to name some places they've traveled to.
- Ask *Did anyone have an embarrassing moment because you weren't aware of a custom?* Elicit an answer or provide an example of your own.
- Ask *Why is it useful to know the customs of a place you have never been to?*
- Students form groups of three or four to discuss.

Wrap-up
Students complete their KWL Charts.
- Students take out their KWL Charts from the Warm-up and complete the final column.
- Students form small groups of three or four and share what they have learned.
- Encourage students to discuss some of the following questions:
  » What was the most interesting thing you learned?
  » What was the most surprising thing you learned?
  » Would you like to go to South Korea? Why or why not?
- Monitor, offering help as needed.
- Come together as a class and have some students share their thoughts and ideas.

➡ **(No homework today.)**

🐝 Teaching Tip
Reading Aloud to Build Comprehension
Reading aloud is a strategy that motivates students, whether it's you or them reading. When someone reads aloud, students tend to focus better on the text, following every word. Students are less likely to get hung up on new vocabulary, and focus on overall meaning. Also, this allows you to control the amount of time students spend with a text.

Lesson 8   Student's Book p. 91

Warm-up

Students play a game of *Casino* to review a text and generate interest.

- Students form pairs. Tell pairs they have $500 to bet; the maximum bet is $100.
- Explain that you will tell them some customs about Korea. Students decide if they think the statement is true or false, and they bet according to how sure they are.
- Pairs keep track of their winnings and losses.
- The pair with the most money wins.
- Here are some statements:
    » *It is impolite to shake hands in Korea.* (False. Men often bow and shake hands.)
    » *Avoid touching or patting a Korean.* (True)
    » *Always pass and receive items with your left hand.* (False. Use your right hand.)
    » *Never pour your own drink. Someone will pour it for you.* (True.)
    » *You should unwrap a gift in front of the giver and say thank you.* (False. Don't open a gift in front of the giver.)

3 Read the blog again. Circle *T* (True) or *F* (False).

Students reread the blog and determine whether the statements are true or false.

Answers

1. F (Madison was born in the US and lived there as a baby.), 2. F (Koreans wear special slippers in school.), 3. T, 4. F (Koreans use the whole hand.), 5. T, 6. F (She sat at the front of the bus.)

4 Think Fast! Name five tips you would give a friend that will visit your country for the first time.

Students do a five-minute timed challenge: they think of five tips for someone visiting their country, using the blog in Activity 2 as a model.

Answers

Answers will vary.

5 Complete the comment to Madison's blog with the words in the box.

Students complete the sentences with the words given.

Answers

1. cultures, 2. age, 3. royalty, 4. eyes, 5. mistakes, 6. socks

Extension

Students make brochures to explain cultural differences.

- Students form groups and decide on a particular culture they wish to research.
- Students conduct research on various aspects of cultural awareness such as greetings, meals, gestures, off-limit topics, attitudes about time, etc.
- Students prepare a brochure that gives tips for a traveler to their chosen country.
- Be sure to display the brochures in your classroom.

Wrap-up

Students discuss their reaction to a text.

- Draw students' attention to the blogs in Activity 2 and Activity 5.
- Write the following questions on the board:
    » *Do you think Madison's tips are useful? Why or why not?*
    » *Are there any similar tips that would be useful for visitors to your country?*
    » *What could Madison have done to avoid a "hard homecoming"?*
- Students form groups of three or four to discuss the questions.
- Monitor, offering help as needed.
- Come together as a class and have some students share their thoughts and ideas.

➧ **(No homework today.)**

> **Objective**
> Students will be able to use phrases to agree or disagree to have a class debate about social media.

Lesson 9   Student's Book p. 92

Warm-up

Students play a game of *Word-in-a-Word* to generate interest.
- Write the word *TEENAGER* on the board.
- Students form pairs.
- Set a stopwatch for one or two minutes.
- Pairs write as many words as they can with the letters in *teenager*.
- When the stopwatch goes off, have pairs take turns reading out their words. If students have the same words, they cross them out.
- When all words have been read, the pair with the most words wins.

1 In pairs, read the comments. Discuss the ones that you agree with.

Students read the comments with a partner and discuss those that they agree with.

Answers
Answers will vary.

2 🎧³¹ Read the responses below. Write the correct letter to each comment in Activity 1. Then listen and check.

Students read the responses and match each to the corresponding comment in Activity 1.

Answers
top to bottom 1. f, 2. g, 3. i, 4. c, 5. b, 6. h, 7. d, 8. a, 9. e

---

Audio Script

1. A: Parents today have no time for their children. They're always working.
   B: That's absolutely right. That's why many people's grandparents look after the kids.
2. A: Smartphones are terrible. I feel anxious whenever I get a message or a tweet.
   B: I totally disagree. Mine is essential. I need to be connected to the Internet all the time.
3. A: There's too much violence on TV.
   B: I agree. There's blood everywhere. It's horrible.
4. A: It's a man's world. We need equal rights for men and women.
   B: I agree up to a point, but things are better for women today than in the past.
5. You can't hang out outside anymore because it's too dangerous.
   B: I disagree. Where I live we do it all the time and we've never had an incident.
6. A: Parents do not have the right to monitor their teenager's activities online.
   B: I partly agree, but sometimes they need to protect their children.
7. A: Teenagers should not wear a school uniform.
   B: I see your point, but it is more expensive for parents to spend so much money on clothes.
8. A: Nobody cares about bullying at school.
   B: I don't think that's true because if you tell any teacher, they will stop it.
9. A: People in my neighborhood care about the environment.
   B: I think that's right. Everyone separates waste, for example.

---

3 Write the phrases in bold in Activity 2 in the correct columns.

Students classify the phrases in Activity 2 used to agree, to disagree and to partly agree.

Answers
Phrases to Agree I think that's right. That's absolutely right. I agree. *Phrases to Disagree* I don't think that's true. I disagree. I totally disagree. *Phrases to Partly Agree* I agree up to a point, but… I see your point, but… I partly agree, but…

Stop and Think! Critical Thinking

What are the biggest worries that teenagers have today in your country: at school, at home, in society?
- Elicit the dilemmas the teens have read about in the unit.
- Ask *What are the biggest worries that teenagers have today?*
- Students form small groups to discuss.
- Elicit the biggest worries as a class.

Wrap-up

Students play a card game to practice response phrases.
- Students form pairs and take out a piece of paper and cut or tear it into nine cards.
- They write the phrases from Activity 2 on the cards, shuffle and deal them out.
- The first student reads a phrase from Activity 1. The other student turns over a card and uses the phrase to respond appropriately.
- Students switch roles.
- Monitor, offering help as needed.

Lesson 10   Student's Book p. 93

Warm-up
Students play a game of *Taboo* to activate prior knowledge and generate interest.
- Students form three groups.
- Each group chooses a student to sit in the "hot seat." This student's back is to the board.
- Write a type of social media on the board, for example, *Facebook, Twitter, LinkedIn, YouTube, Instagram, flickr, tumblr, Google hangouts.*
- The other students describe the social media, trying to get the students in the hot seat to guess the word without saying it.
- Once a student has guessed the word, award that group a point, have groups choose another student to sit in the hot seat and write another type of social media.
- Continue as long as time permits and students are engaged.

4 You will have a class debate. In your notebook, follow the steps to get ready.

Students choose sides in the debate—they decide if they are for or against the statement: *When using social media, we're giving up our privacy.* Then they follow the steps to generate ideas for their debate.

Answers

Answers will vary.

5 Think Fast! Name the three most popular social media in your country.

Students do a one-minute timed challenge: they list the three most popular social media.

Answers

Answers will vary.

6 Work in small groups with classmates who share your opinion. In your notebook, follow the steps.

Students follow the steps in groups of people who share their opinion about privacy and social media. They prepare their argument to defend their opinion.

7 Work with a group that doesn't share your opinion on the topic. Follow the steps to have a debate.

Groups with opposing opinions hold a debate.

The Digital Touch
To incorporate digital media in the project, suggest one or more of the following:
- Read about different debate formats: goo.gl/FD5ev9.
- Organize your debate online: goo.gl/uGsPzx.

Note that students should have the option to do a task on paper or digitally.

Wrap-up
Students reflect on the debate.
- One student from each group meets with others to form new groups.
- Students discuss the following:
  » *What did you like most about the debate?*
  » *What did you like least?*
  » *What was the most interesting idea to come from the other side?*
  » *Would you change anything about your debate? If so, what?*

➡ **Workbook p. 148, Activity 1 (Review)**

Teaching Tip
Using Peer-Teaching
Learning a foreign language, even if its roots are familiar, is a very daunting task for students of any age. Learning it alone is even more difficult. To make your students feel comfortable practicing their new language, get them to work in pairs or larger groups so that they can help each other. Lessons become fun, and communicating and learning English becomes more natural when students can work through it together and peer-teach.

Review

Objectives
Students will be able to consolidate their understanding of **phrasal verbs** and **modals of possibility**.

Lesson 11   Student's Book p. 94

> ✔ Homework Check!
> Workbook p. 148, Activity 1
> **Answers**
> **1 Unscramble the sentences.**
> 1. Mike and Kelly may break up even though they get along well. 2. Despite the counseling, Sally could not get over her parents' divorce.
> 3. You could just keep it to yourself. 4. She might apologize and own up.

Warm-up
Students play a game of *Go Fish* to review phrasal verbs.
- Have students take out the cards they made from the Wrap-up in Lesson 1.
- Students form groups of four. They put their cards together and shuffle them.
- One student deals out five cards to each student. The rest of the cards go into a pile, which is the "pond."
- The student asks the student to the left of him for a card that matches one of the cards in his hand. If the student has the card, she gives it to him and he asks the student next to her for another card. If not, she says, "Go fish," and the student draws a card from the pile. If he draws a match, he continues play; if not, the play goes to the student on his left.
- Students play until all phrasal verbs are matched up. The student with the most pairs wins.

1 Match the captions to the pictures.
Students review phrasal verbs by matching the sentences to the corresponding pictures.
Answers
1. d, 2. a, 3. b, 4. c

2 Match the sentence halves.
Students form phrasal verbs to correctly match the beginnings and endings of the sentences.
Answers
1. d, 2. c, 3. b, 4. a

3 Complete the dialogues with the phrasal verbs in the box.
Students determine which phrasal verb correctly completes each sentence.
Answers
1. figure out, 2. own up, 3. break up, 4. get along with, 5. tell on, 6. give up, 7. get over, 8. keep it to, 9. turn him in, 10. go on

Wrap-up
Students play a game of *Charades* to review phrasal verbs.
- Students form groups of three and take turns acting out phrasal verbs without speaking.
- Students keep track of how many phrasal verbs they guess correctly.
- Set a stopwatch for five minutes.
- When the stopwatch goes off, the team who has guessed the most phrasal verbs wins.

➡ **(No homework today.)**

🐝 Teaching Tip
Using Graphic Organizers to Review
Encourage students to use different types of graphic organizers to study the material. For example, they can use a topic wheel or mind map to organize cultural tips. Students can use a Venn diagram or word cluster to organize phrasal verbs. Students can do this at home and then bring in their organizers and share them with the class. The act of preparing the organizer is the first part of their review; then presenting it to their classmates gives students another chance for review.

Lesson 12   Student's Book p. 95

Warm-up
Students play a guessing game to review modal verbs of possibility.
- Students take out a piece of paper and write down a place. It can be a city, country, landmark or location, but each student should write the same type of place.
- Collect the papers and redistribute them.
- Students form pairs and write sentences, using the modals *can / can't, might / might not, could / couldn't, may / may not,* to describe the place. Students shouldn't state the place in the sentences.
- Pairs take turns reading their sentences to the class. Others try to guess the place.

4 Unscramble the sentences.
Students determine word order to form sentences expressing degrees of possibility.

Answers
1. We could have a surprise quiz tomorrow. 2. My brother may leave home next year. 3. Your soccer team might win the league. 4. We can't get a bus to the city center. 5. Sam may be grounded because he skipped history class.

5 In pairs, look at the extreme close-ups and discuss what they are. Use *might, could* or *may*.
Students discuss what the pictures might be using modal verbs of possibility.

Answers
1. a lizard, 2. sand, 3. a basketball, 4. a mushroom, 5. a fly's eye, 6. a slice of tomato

Big Question
Students are given the opportunity to revisit the Big Question and reflect on it.
- Ask students to turn to the unit opener on page 83 and think about the question *Why do we behave the way we do?*
- Ask students to think about the discussions they've about moral dilemmas, the readings they've read, the texts they've listened to and the debate they had.
- Students form small groups to discuss the following:
  » *Is it easy to accept people that are different from us?*
  » *How do you react when your parents ground you?*
  » *How do teachers in your school react to bullying?*
  » *Have you ever been bullied in social media? If so, what did you do?*
  » *How do mobile devices affect our face-to-face interactions?*
- Monitor, offering help as needed, particularly with vocabulary.

⭐ Scorecard
Hand out (and/or project) a *Scorecard*. Have students fill in their *Scorecards* for this unit.

➡️ **Study for the unit test.**

7 What's it like in your country?

Grammar	Vocabulary
The Passive, Present and Past (+,-,?): Polka dots <u>are worn</u> by everyone. The noodles <u>were cooked</u> by Lisa's grandpa.	**Food Around the World:** acarajé, baklava, British lunch, ceviche, dim sum, goulash, tandoori chicken **Cooking Verbs:** baking, boiling, frying, grilling, roasting, steaming **Adjectives:** bland, chewy, crispy, raw, sour, spicy, sticky

Listening	Writing
Identifying supporting information	Using correct capitalization and punctuation

What's it like in your country?

In the first lesson, read the unit title aloud and have students look carefully at the unit cover. Encourage them to think about the message in the picture. At the end of the unit, students will discuss the big question: *What's it like in your country?*

Teaching Tip
Building Choice into Your Classroom

While you cannot simply let students choose what they want to do, you can integrate choice as a strategy within your lesson. To do this, first identify the main objective of your task. (That is not up for choice!) Once your main objective is clear, think of various ways of achieving it. The choice can be the type of task, grouping or the way to present it, among others. Here are some examples:

- If students are doing a writing assignment, provide a few alternative topics.
- If you are reviewing vocabulary or grammar, write two different task types for the same concept.
- If students are presenting on a topic, let them choose the tool. PowerPoint? A video? A poster?

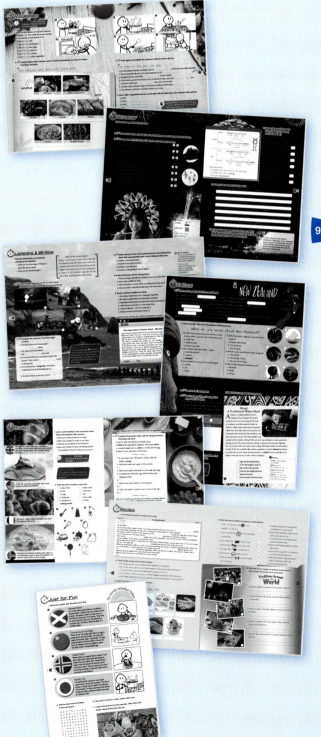

# Vocabulary

Objectives
Students will be able to use **food around the world, cooking verbs** and **adjectives** vocabulary to talk about food in different countries.

Lesson 1 — Student's Book pp. 98 and 99

Warm-up
Students play a game of *Call My Bluff* to generate interest and activate prior knowledge.
- Draw students' attention to the photos on page 97.
- Students form groups of three. They try to guess what the places are in the photos. If they don't know a place, they try to convince the other members of their group of the place by giving context.
- Monitor, offering help as needed.
- When students have finished, come together as a class and see how many know the places. *(from left to right)* macaroons made in France, Chinese New Year parade, New Year's Eve at Times Square in New York City, Day of the Dead in Mexico, scorpions and seahorses on sticks eaten as snacks in China, river market in Asia, the Colosseum in Rome, Italy)

 100

1 Think Fast! In your notebook, write four types of: meat, fish, fruit and vegetables.
Students do a three-minute timed challenge: they list types of food to activate prior knowledge.

Answers

Answers will vary.

2 Read the descriptions of what Mr. Stickman is doing (1–6). Then write the correct number of the description in each picture (a–f).
Students match cooking verbs vocabulary with illustrations of each method.

Answers

1. d, 2. c, 3. e, 4. b, 5. f, 6. a

3 🎧32 Label the dishes below with the words in the box that indicate how they are cooked. Then listen and check.
Students learn about different dishes and identify the cooking methods used to prepare them.

Answers

1. steamed, 2. roasted, 3. boiled, 4. fried, 5. baked, 6. (raw) not cooked, 7. grilled

Audio Script
1. Dim sum are traditional dumplings from China. They are usually steamed. There are many different varieties of dim sum, but they are usually savory, not sweet. They often contain meat like beef or chicken.
2. The stereotype of British cooking is that it's bland and doesn't taste like anything. However, Sunday lunch is a special meal. The classic is roast beef. It's usually served with a meat sauce called gravy.
3. Goulash is a thick meat soup from Hungary. To make it, you boil beef or lamb with garlic, onion, carrots and peppers. There are usually big pieces of meat in goulash, so it's chewy.
4. Acarajé is a popular type of street food in Brazil. It's made from beans which are fried in oil. You then cut it in half and add a filling of shrimps or peppers. Acarajé is lovely and a little crispy on the outside.
5. Baklava is a popular dessert from Turkey. You make pastry with cheese and honey. You then bake it in the oven. At the end, you pour more honey on it, so baklava is very sweet and sticky, too.
6. Ceviche is a seafood dish from Peru. Ceviche is made with raw fish, so it's served cold. Ceviche is also covered in juice from lemons and limes, which taste sour.
7. Tandoori chicken is from India. The chicken is covered in red chili powder, so it is very spicy. Then the chicken is grilled and served with a creamy sauce made with yogurt.

Wrap-up
Students play a game of *Pictionary* to review vocabulary.
- Students form groups of three or four.
- Set a stopwatch for three minutes.
- A student draws one of the phrases from the vocabulary. He / She is not allowed to speak or write words, only draw pictures.
- Once a student guesses the phrase, a different student draws another one.
- When the stopwatch goes off, the group with the most correctly guessed vocabulary items wins.

➡ **Workbook pp. 150 and 151, Activities 3–5**

Lesson 2   Student's Book p. 99

✔ **Homework Check!**
Workbook pp. 150 and 151, Activities 3–5
Answers
3 Write the names of the dishes.
1. Acarajé, 2. Tandoori chicken, 3. Goulash,
4. Dim sum, 5. British Sunday lunch, 6. Ceviche
4 Correct one mistake in each sentence.
1. ~~bake~~ At a barbeque it's common to <u>grill</u> meat.
2. ~~grill~~ My family likes to <u>boil</u> eggs in water instead of frying them in oil. 3. ~~fries~~ My aunt <u>bakes</u> some great cakes and pies. 4. ~~roast~~ I can't cook! The only thing I can do is <u>boil</u> water. 5. ~~baked~~ My favorite food at a Chinese restaurant is the <u>steamed</u> rice with eggs and vegetables.
5 Complete the description of each dish from Activity 3.
1. Dim sum, 2. Ceviche, 3. Tandoori chicken,
4. Acarajé, 5. Baklava, 6. Goulash

Warm-up
Students review dishes with a game of *Hangman*.
• Draw a hangman's noose, like this, on the board:

• Choose one of the dishes from Activity 3, for example, *dim sum*, and write the same number of blanks as there are in the word on the board:

___ ___ ___ / ___ ___ ___

• Students form two or three teams. Team members take turns calling out letters. If a student calls out a letter that is part of the word, for example, *d*, write that letter in the appropriate blank or blanks. If it is not part of the word, draw the person on the noose, beginning with the head. Draw one part of the body for each letter called that is not part of the word. Be sure to write the called-out letter to the side so that students don't call it out again.
• The game is over when teams have either guessed the word, completed the word, or the body is complete.
• If time permits, have a student come up and choose a dish, while others call out letters and try to guess. Award points for correct guesses.

4 🎧³² **Listen again and complete the sentences with the words in the box.**
Students complete the descriptions of the dishes with the appropriate adjectives from the listening.
Answers
1. bland, 2. chewy, 3. crispy, 4. sticky, 5. raw,
6. sour, 7. spicy

5 Write a dish or ingredient that you can describe with the following words. Compare with a partner.
Students use the adjectives to describe dishes they are familiar with and share their descriptions in pairs.
Answers
Answers will vary.

6 In pairs, take turns answering the questions about Activity 3.
Students discuss their answers to the questions listed about the dishes described in Activity 3.
Answers
Answers will vary.

Stop and Think! Critical Thinking
What dish from your country is identified around the world? What does it taste like?
• Have students name some dishes from their country/ies.
• Ask *Do you like [name of dish]? Why or why not?*
• Then ask *What dish from your country is identified around the world? What does it taste like?*
• Students form small groups to discuss.

> **Extension**
> Students do a "taste test" to personalize the lesson.
> • Bring in various types of food that will elicit the different tastes.
> • Students put on blindfolds and say how the food tastes.

Wrap-up
Students play a game of *Memory* to review vocabulary.
• Students form pairs and take out a piece of paper, which cut or tear into seven pieces.
• One student writes the words to describe taste and texture from Activity 5, one on each card. Together, they write a corresponding food item for each word on the other cards.
• They shuffle the cards and place them face-down between them.
• Students take turns turning over two cards at a time, trying to match the taste or texture with the corresponding food.
• The student with the most matches wins.

➡ **Workbook p. 150, Activities 1 and 2**

Objective
Students will be able to use **the passive, present and past** to talk about traditions.

Lesson 3   Student's Book p. 100

✔ **Homework Check!**
Workbook p. 150, Activities 1 and 2
Answers
1 Match the sentences.
top to bottom 2, 5, 0, 3, 1, 4
2 Write the words below next to the food item that they describe.
1. chewy, 2. salty, 3. sour, 4. bland, 5. sticky

Warm-up
Students play a game called *Word-in-a-Word* to generate interest.
- Write the words *NEW YEAR* on the board.
- Students form pairs.
- Set a stopwatch for one or two minutes.
- Pairs write as many words as they can with the letters in *New Year*.
- When the stopwatch goes off, pairs take turns reading out their words. If students have the same words, they cross them out.
- When all words have been read, the pair with the most words wins.

 102

1 Discuss these questions with a partner.
Students work in pairs to discuss the questions about how they celebrated the last New Year.

2 🎧³³ Listen to Erin talk about her last New Year. Write her answers to the questions in Activity 1.
Students listen to the conversation and answer the questions in the previous activity from Erin's perspective.
Answers
1. At my friend Lisa's apartment. 2. Lisa's family. 3. Noodles and lots of different food. 4. Lisa's grandpa, 5. yes

Audio Script
HUGH: Where did you celebrate the last New Year, Erin?
ERIN: My friend Lisa invited me and my brother to her home. We celebrated last New Year at her apartment.
HUGH: Who were you with?
ERIN: We were with Lisa's family. They're from the Philippines.
HUGH: What did you eat?
ERIN: I ate noodles and lots of different food. It was delicious.
HUGH: Who cooked?
ERIN: The food was cooked by Lisa's grandpa. He's an amazing cook.
HUGH: Did you have fun?
ERIN: Yes! It was the best New Year of my life!

3 🎧³⁴ Listen and cross (✘) T (True) or F (False). Correct the false information.
Students listen to the rest of the conversation and determine whether passive voice statements about the listening are true or false.
Answers
1. F; My <u>brother</u> and I were invited to the party. 2. T, 3. F; At New Year in the Philippines, all the <u>kids</u> jump high in the air. 4. T, 5. F; The noodles are long, so they are said to represent long <u>life</u>. 6. T, 7. T

Audio Script
HUGH: So what is New Year like with a Filipino family?
ERIN: Amazing. My brother and I were invited to the party and everyone was really nice to us.
HUGH: Do they have any special traditions for New Year?
ERIN: They have a lot of traditions! Firstly, polka dots are worn by everyone. The dots are circles. Circles are thought to bring prosperity because they look like coins.
HUGH: Cool! I never wear polka dots!
ERIN: Another tradition is ... uhm ... At New Year in the Philippines, all the kids jump high in the air when the clock strikes 12. It's believed that if you jump high, you'll grow tall!
HUGH: Ha ha! Great! So what did you eat?
ERIN: I was given some amazing noodles. The noodles were cooked by Lisa's grandpa. He is 82! Noodles are eaten by Filipinos at New Year. The noodles are long, so they are said to represent long life!
HUGH: Yum, yum! We eat fish at New Year.
ERIN: Well, in the Philippines, chicken and fish aren't eaten at New Year's Eve. It's bad luck on that day—they are thought to represent scarcity of food.
HUGH: Are there any other traditions?
ERIN: Yes, the house isn't cleaned on New Year's Eve. It is thought you sweep all the good luck out of your house!
HUGH: I like that tradition! My parents always clean the house on New Year's!

Wrap-up
Students discuss how they celebrate New Year's.
- Students form small groups and discuss how they celebrate New Year's in their country/ies and families.
- Monitor, offering help as needed.
- Come together as a class and have some students share their thoughts and ideas.

 Workbook p. 151, Activities 1 and 2

> 💭 **Teaching Tip**
> **Withholding Correction to Promote Fluency**
> Focusing on accuracy is often at the cost of fluency. Consider this when your students are discussing or role-playing freely, without being hyperaware of their accuracy.

Lesson 4   Student's Book p. 101

> ✔ **Homework Check!**
> Workbook p. 151, Activities 1 and 2
>
> **Answers**
> **1 Underline the verb and label each sentence A (Active) or P (Passive).**
> 1. P, 2. A, 3. P, 4. P, 5. A
> **2 Underline the correct option to complete the text.**
> 1. make, 2. was, 3. were boiled, 4. baked, 5. were steamed, 6. baked

Warm-up

Students review the listening with a race.
- Before class, draw images of the following on the board: *a bowl of noodles, polka dots, the number 12, chicken and fish, a broom.*
- When students enter, they form groups of three.
- The first group to state correctly what each image means wins.

4 Focus on the uses of the passive. Write A (Action), U (Unknown) or NI (not important).

Students read passive voice sentences and determine whether the passive is used because the action is more important than the doer, the doer is unknown or the doer is not important.

Answers

1. A, 2. NI, 3. A, 4. NI, 5. U, 6. A

5 Change these sentences into the passive.

Students read active voice sentences and rewrite them in passive voice.
- Draw students' attention to **The Passive** box and read the information aloud. Explain how the subject and object in an active sentence exchange places in the passive. Provide further explanation of the three uses of the passive if necessary.
- Students rewrite the sentences.

Answers

1. In Denmark, plates are often broken to celebrate New Year. 2. Red is often worn at New Year in my country. 3. In Spain, twelve grapes are eaten at midnight at New Year. 4. In Scotland, the traditional song "Auld Lang Syne" is sung at New Year. 5. The New Year's party was held by my family last year. 6. In Greece, a coin is put in a New Year's cake for good luck.

6 In your notebook, compare New Year in your country with New Year in the Philippines. Write sentences using the passive. Look at the example to help you.

Using the ideas in the wrap-up in the previous lesson, students write a paragraph about their own New Year using the paragraph of the New Year's in China as a model. Monitor that students use the passive voice and provide help as necessary.

Wrap-up

Students play a game of *Snap* to review the passive voice.
- Have each student take out two pieces of paper and cut or tear them into 14 cards.
- Each student chooses seven sentences from pages 100 and 101 and writes them on individual cards.
- Students form pairs. They help each other write the sentences, in either passive or active voice, on the rest of the cards.
- Students put their cards together, shuffle them and deal them out.
- At the same time, pairs turn over one card. If the cards are the active and passive form of the same sentence, a student slaps his hand on the set of cards and says, "Snap!"
- Students play until all cards are matched. The student with the most cards wins.

▶ **Workbook p. 152, Activities 3 and 4**

Listening & Writing

Objectives
Students will be able to identify supporting information and use correct capitalization and punctuation.

Lesson 5 Student's Book pp. 102 and 103

> ✔ Homework Check!
> Workbook p. 152, Activities 3 and 4
> **Answers**
> **3 Complete the sentences in the present or past passive using the verbs below.**
> 1. was stolen, 2. was invited, 3. is cleaned, 4. is cooked, 5. are baked
> **4 Read the sentences and choose when the doer is not important (*NI*) or when the doer is unknown (*U*).**
> 1. NI, 2. U, 3. NI, 4. NI, 5. U

Warm-up
Students make a KWL Chart to preview the topic.
• Draw a KWL Chart on the board, similar to following:

What I Know	What I Want to Know	What I Have Learned

• Ask students to think about what they know about Easter Island and what they want to know.
• Tell students they will read about Easter Island.

1 Read the introduction to an interview and discuss the questions.
Students read the paragraph and discuss what's it like to live in a place like Easter Island in small groups.

2 🎧³⁵ Listen to Diego talk about his life on Easter Island. Number the pictures in the order they are mentioned.
Students listen to the interview and identify the order the topics.

Answer
top row 4, 1, *bottom row* 2, 3

Audio Script

INTERVIEWER: Diego, what's it like in your country?
DIEGO: Well, my country is Chile and I live on Easter Island.
INTERVIEWER: What do you like about Easter Island?
DIEGO: First of all, it's world famous. Everyone knows our famous giant stone heads. There are around 1,000. Some are 10 meters high!
INTERVIEWER: Is life boring on Easter Island?
DIEGO: No! People are very happy here. We smile a lot. The best moment in the year is the Tapati Festival.
INTERVIEWER: What's the Tapati Festival?
DIEGO: The Tapati Festival is held in January and February each year. It's a mix of ancient sports, carnival and theater presentations. It's a lot of fun.
INTERVIEWER: Sounds great. So are there any special dishes on Easter Island?
DIEGO: Our most famous dish is umu.
INTERVIEWER: Umu? What is it?
DIEGO: To cook it, you make a hole in the ground. Then, meat or fish is put in the ground and they are roasted with vegetables and fruit wrapped in banana leaves, like in an oven. It takes a long time to cook, but it's delicious!
INTERVIEWER: Yum! So, final question. What hobbies do you have?
DIEGO: I love astronomy – stargazing. I was given a telescope for my birthday by my parents and I'm hooked.
INTERVIEWER: Why do you like it?
DIEGO: On Easter Island, there isn't a lot of electric light. This means that you can see the stars very clearly.
INTERVIEWER: So you don't go to bed early?
DIEGO: No, I'm allowed to stay up till midnight on the weekends!
INTERVIEWER: Wow! Nice parents! Diego, thanks for talking to us.
DIEGO: Gracias a ustedes! Thank you!

3 🎧³⁵ Complete the sentences. Then listen again to check.
Students complete the sentences with words from the listening.
• Ask students to complete the sentences.
• Draw students' attention to the **Guess What!** box. Tell them that in 2012, archaeologists excavated a couple of giant heads and discovered they actually have bodies! They are standing figures with torsos from the waist up that were buried by dirt over the centuries.

Answer
1. stone, 2. January, February, 3. fish, 4. parents, 5. electric light

4 🎧³⁵ Work in groups of four. Each student listens for more information about their corresponding topic. In your notebook, take notes.
Students identify supporting information.
• Draw students' attention to the **Be Strategic!** box and read the information aloud.

Answer
Answers will vary.

Wrap-up
Students complete their KWL Charts.
• Students complete the final column of their KWL Charts.
• Encourage students to discuss:
  » *What was the most surprising thing you learned? Would you like to go to Easter Island? Why or why not?*

➡ **Workbook p. 153, Activities 1 and 2**

Lesson 6 — Student's Book p. 103

✔ **Homework Check!**
Workbook p. 153, Activities 1 and 2
Answers
1 Circle the types of cooking food that are popular in your community.
Answers will vary.
2 Read the text. Then mark each statement T (True) or F (False). In your notebook, correct the false statements.
1. F; Eating burned food can increase your risk of cancer. 2. F; Peppers and onions are better for you if you eat them raw. 3. T, 4. T

Warm-up
Students test their knowledge of a place to activate prior knowledge and generate interest.
- Write *Easter Island* on the board.
- Students form teams of three or four and come to the board.
- Tell students you will say some facts about Easter Island. If they think the statement is true, they write *T* on the board; if they think it's false, they write *F*.
- Say the following statements:
  » *Easter Island is in Asia. (False. It's in South America.)*
  » *Easter Island is in the Pacific Ocean. (True)*
  » *Easter Island is only around 25 km (15 m) long. (True)*
  » *There are thousands of statues on Easter Island. (False. There are fewer than 900.)*
  » *The statues are made out of ash from volcanoes. (True)*
- Tell students the answers. The group with the most correct guesses wins.

5 In the same groups, discuss the questions.
Students discuss their experience of working on the listening skills (identifying supporting information) in Activity 4 in their groups.
Answer
Answers will vary.

6 Read six common mistakes in writing.
Students read information about common mistakes in punctuation and capitalization.

7 Read the text and find the mistakes described in Activity 6. Then correct them.
Students identify and correct the punctuation and capitalization mistakes in the text using the list of common mistakes in Activity 6.
Answer
1. ~~french~~, French, 2. ~~brazilian~~, Brazilian, 3. a ~~surfers~~ paradise, a surfer's paradise, 4. ~~Its~~ big, It's big,
5. very friendly… 6. first paragraph

Stop and Think! Critical Thinking
What is the difference between an exclamation mark (!), an ellipsis (…) and a period (.)? Which one do we use most in writing?
- Have students find examples of exclamation marks (!), ellipses (…) and periods (.) in the Student's Book.
- Ask *What's the difference between them?*
- Students form small groups and discuss.
- Students should express that we use an exclamation mark to show a strong and intense statement or command; an ellipsis is used to show that some information is missing, or there is a pause or break; and a period is used to show that a sentence has ended. We use periods most in writing.

> **Extension**
> Students do further research on their topics and present it to the class.
> - Students work in their groups from Activity 4. They do further research on their topics.
> - Students present their topics to the class. Encourage them to use visual aids.

Wrap-up
Students play a game called *The Dot Game* to review common mistakes.
- Draw 25 dots in a square on the board similar to the following:

- Students form groups of five or six and are assigned numbers: Team 1, Team 2, Team 3, etc.
- Write a sentence with a mistake similar to the ones in Activity 7.
- If the first student in the group identifies the mistake, he / she draws a horizontal or diagonal line between two dots. If the student answers incorrectly or doesn't know, the next team gets a chance.
- The students continue drawing lines, one by one, between the dots until a team makes a square. Then the team writes their number.
- The team with the most squares on the board wins.

➡ **Workbook p. 153, Activity 3**

Preparing for the Next Lesson
Ask students to watch an introduction to New Zealand: goo.gl/9jxf7D or invite them look at the website goo.gl/VxWny8.

 Culture

Objectives
Students will be able to use **cooking verbs** and vocabulary as well as practice listening for supporting information.

Lesson 7 Student's Book pp. 104 and 105

✔ Homework Check!
Workbook p. 153, Activity 3
Answers
3 In your notebook, answer the following questions. Then use that information to write a reflection on how food is prepared in your family.
Answers will vary.

Warm-up
Students compare what they know about New Zealand and Easter Island.
- Students form pairs and brainstorm what they learned about Easter Island.
- Then they brainstorm what they know about New Zealand.
- Draw a Venn diagram on the board. Write *New Zealand* over one circle and *Easter Island* over the other.
- Students form pairs and draw a similar diagram. They write any similarities between the countries in the overlapping part. Other information goes in the corresponding circles.
- Students get together with another pair to compare their diagrams.
- Tell students they will add more to their diagrams after the lesson.

1 🎧³⁶ **Listen and complete the fact file on New Zealand.**
Students listen to the information about New Zealand and complete the sentences with words from the listening.
Answers
1. Southern, 2. London, 3. capital, 4. 4.5, 5. Fifteen, 6. Holland

Audio Script
New Zealand is in the Southern Hemisphere. On maps, it is often placed near Australia, but actually, they are 4,155 kilometers apart. That's almost the distance between London and Iraq.
There are two main islands in New Zealand: North Island and South Island. Most people live in North Island, which is where the capital, Wellington, is, as well as the largest city, Auckland.
About 4.5 million people live in New Zealand. Fifteen percent of them are Maori—the original inhabitants of the islands before the Europeans arrived. Its name comes from Zeeland, which is a region in Holland.

2 **Answer the quiz. Then match the questions with the pictures.**
Students learn about New Zealand as they complete the quiz and match the questions to the photos.
Answers
left column 6, 3, 4, *right column* 1, 2, 5

3 🎧³⁷ **Listen to check your answers.**
Students listen to the interview and check their answers to the quiz in Activity 2.
Answers
1. b, 2. c, 3. a, 4. c, 5. a, c, 6. b

Audio Script
HANK: So Kylie, let's look at the answers to the New Zealand quiz.
KYLIE: Sure, Hank.
HANK: Question 1. In 1893, New Zealand became the first country in the world to give the vote in elections to … ?
KYLIE: All adult women. Answer B. 1893! By comparison, women only got the vote in the United States in 1920.
HANK: OK. Question 2. New Zealand has the world's "blank" street.
KYLIE: Answer C. Steepest street. It's Baldwin Street and in the steepest section it has a 38 percent grade angle! A race is held there every year.
HANK: Number 3. New Zealand is home to the world's largest …
KYLIE: This is amazing, Hank. It's the cricket. Answer A. It's a type of weta, but it can't jump.
HANK: A cricket that can't jump …
KYLIE: And it has ears on its knees. Can you believe it?
HANK: Wow! Now, number 4. Which kiwi didn't originally come from New Zealand?
KYLIE: This is the kiwi fruit. Answer C. It was brought to New Zealand from China.
HANK: And people?
KYLIE: In slang, people from New Zealand are called "kiwis." Like me, I'm a kiwi.
HANK: Right. Number 5. Which movies were filmed in New Zealand? I know this. It's answer A. The Hobbit.
KYLIE: That's right. The Hobbit was filmed in New Zealand. Do you remember The Lord of the Rings films? They were also filmed in New Zealand. Answer C.
HANK: And finally, what is New Zealand's national sport?
KYLIE: It's answer B. Rugby. The New Zealand rugby team are known as "The All Blacks."
HANK: Thanks so much, Kylie. I've learned a lot today!

Wrap-up
Students complete their Venn diagrams.
- Students meet with their partners from the Warm-up.
- They complete their diagrams.
- Monitor, offering help as needed.
- Come together as a class and have students compare their diagrams.

➡ **(No homework today.)**

Lesson 8   Student's Book p. 105

Warm-up
Students race to review facts about New Zealand.
- Students form three or four teams and line up in front of the board.
- Give the first student of each group a marker.
- Ask questions about the text. Students race to write the answers on the board. The group that is first to write the correct answer is awarded a point.
- Here are some questions you can ask:
    » *Which hemisphere is New Zealand on? (Southern)*
    » *How far is New Zealand from Australia? (4.155 km)*
    » *What are the main islands' names? (North Island and South Island)*
    » *What is the capital of New Zealand? (Wellington)*
    » *What is the largest city? (Auckland)*
    » *How many people live in New Zealand? (4.5 million)*
    » *What percent of them are Maori? (15%)*
    » *Which country does the name New Zealand come from? (Holland)*

4 **Work in groups of three. Listen again for supporting information.**

Students listen to the interview again and practice listening for supporting information and taking notes about their corresponding questions of the quiz.

Answer
Answers will vary.

5 Compare your answers to Activity 4 with another group. Then listen again if necessary.

Students discuss the information they gathered in the previous Activity with another group.
- Ask students to compare the supporting information they gathered with another group.
- Draw students' attention to the **Guess What!** box. Tell them that in New Zealand, only 5% of the population is humans, the rest are animals.

6 Read the text and number the steps below.

Students read the text for specific information about a Maori dish and order the steps in the process.

Answer
3, 5, 1, 6, 4, 2

Wrap-up
Students write a postcard about an imaginary trip.
- Tell students to imagine they took a trip to New Zealand. Ask: *What did you do there? What did you see? What did you eat? Did you enjoy yourself? Would you go back again?*
- Students write postcards about their imaginary trip.
- Come together as a class and have some students share their postcards.

 (No homework today.)

> ### Teaching Tip
> **Building Tolerance in the Classroom**
> Students, like all of us, often impose stereotypes. Ask students about the stereotypes they've personally experienced and open up discussion on tolerance and acceptance. Use some of the topics in the Student's Book, for example, the reading on Maoris, to teach them about tolerance. Ask them to think of all the things that make Maoris (or another culture) different from their culture/s and all the things that are similar. Chances are, there will be more things that are similar (families, schools, goals) than are different. Point this out to your students.

Objective
Students will be able to use **cooking verbs** vocabulary to write a recipe for a popular dish in their country.

Lesson 9   Student's Book pp. 106 and 107

Warm-up
Students brainstorm breakfast foods to activate prior knowledge and generate interest.
- Write *breakfast* on the board.
- Students form groups of three.
- Set a stopwatch.
- Groups list as many types of breakfast foods as they can.
- When the stopwatch goes off, groups take turns reading from their lists. As an item is read, students cross it off their lists.
- Once all items have been read aloud, the group with the most words wins.

1 Look at some breakfasts from around the world. Discuss the questions with a partner.
Students read the information about breakfasts in different countries and discuss the questions.

2 Think Fast! Name the ingredients of your favorite breakfast.
Students do a two-minute timed challenge: they think of their favorite breakfast and list its ingredients.
- Draw students' attention to the **Guess What!** box. Tell them that the English word "dinner" comes from the old French word "disnar," which means "breakfast."
- Ask students to name their favorite ingredients.
- Ask a few volunteers to share their lists with the class.

Answer
Answers will vary.

3 Write the correct number of each item.
Students identify the icons that correspond to the ingredients and tools listed.

Answer
left column 8, 6, 5, 9, 1, *right column* 3, 10, 2, 7, 4

4 In pairs, discuss how to make pancakes with the ingredients in Activity 3.
Students discuss the steps to make pancakes with a partner, using the items listed in Activity 3.

Extension
Students discuss how to make other recipes.
- Students form three groups.
- Each group is assigned one of the dishes on page 106 (except the pancakes because they will learn the recipe in Activity 5 the following class.
- Students discuss how to make their dish.
- Monitor, offering help as needed, particularly with vocabulary.
- Challenge students to write the recipes.

Wrap-up
Students play a game of *Taboo* to review vocabulary.
- Divide the class into two or three groups. Set a chair in front of each group so that the backs are to the board.
- Write one of the words from Activity 3 on the board.
- Each team tries to describe the word to the student in the "hot seat," without using the word or any forms of it.
- Once a student has guessed the word, erase it.
- The student that describes the word successfully gets a point for his / her group.
- Erase the word, have new students sit in the hot seats and write another word on the board.
- Continue until you have reviewed all the words from Activity 3.
- The team with the most points wins.

Lesson 10 Student's Book p. 107

Warm-up
Students play a game of *Simon Says* to review commands.
- Model the activity by saying a command with one of the verbs from Activity 5 and the phrase *Simon says: Simon says, add some flour to the bowl* and mime it.
- Students act out the command.
- Then say a command without the phrase: *Whisk the eggs together*.
- Ask students act out the command, remind them that you did not say *Simon says*, therefore, they should not act it out. You must say *Simon says*, or the students who act out the command sit down and are out of the game.
- Continue saying commands with or without *Simon says*. Use some of the verbs from Activity 5.
- The last student or students standing win the game.

5 🎧³⁸ **Complete the pancake recipe with the missing sentences. Then listen and check.**

Students identify where the sentences go in the pancake recipe and listen to the audio to check their answers.

Answer
c, b, d, a

Audio Script
In one bowl, mix 125 grams of flour with the baking powder.
Add some salt and sugar to the powder.
In another bowl, mix 125 milliliters of milk with the egg.
Melt some butter and add it to the milk and egg.
Combine the milk and egg with the flour and baking powder.
Whisk all the ingredients together. This makes batter.
Melt some more butter in a frying pan.
When it's hot, add some of the batter.
Once one side is cooked, turn it over in the pan.
Serve it with some butter and maple syrup.

6 In small groups, think of a popular dish from your country. Write a recipe for how to make it. Follow the steps.

Using the recipe in Activity 5 as a model, students follow the steps to write their own.

Stop and Think! Critical Thinking
They say "if you can read, you can cook." Do you agree? Why or why not?
- Ask students to share their experiences cooking. Ask *Do you like to cook? Do you cook often? Do you think it's difficult to cook a nice dish?*
- Tell students the maxim *If you can read, you can cook*. Ask *Why do you think people say that? Do you agree? Why or why not?*
- Students form small groups to discuss.

The Digital Touch
To incorporate digital media in the project, suggest one or more of the following:
- Add pictures for your recipe with software like Word or Publisher.
- Make your own recipe book online: goo.gl/LTwGJ2.

Note that students should have the option to do a task on paper or digitally.

Extension
Students have a potluck (a gathering where each guest shares a dish of food) in class.
- Ask students to cook the recipe they came up with in Activity 6 and bring it to class.
- While the class is enjoying the food, challenge students to say what the ingredients are and how they made their dishes.

Wrap-up
Students play a game called *Make That Recipe* to consolidate the lesson.
- Students form groups of three.
- Tell them they are going to make a shopping list. Dictate, or write on the board, the following:
  » *a green vegetable*
  » *another vegetable*
  » *a type of meat or fish*
  » *something spicy*
  » *something sour*
  » *something sticky*
  » *something chewy*
  » *something crispy*
  » *something bland*
- Groups think of one food item for each category.
- When students have finished, collect the lists and redistribute them so that each group has a new list.
- Set a stopwatch for 15 minutes.
- Students have to come up with a recipe using only the ingredients on their list (plus salt, pepper and oil or butter).
- Monitor, offering help as needed.
- When the stopwatch goes off, groups present their recipes.
- Students vote on which dish they would be most willing to eat.

➡ **Workbook p. 152, Activity 1 (Review)**

Review

Objectives
Students will be able to use **cooking verbs** and **adjectives** vocabulary, as well as **present** and **past passive** to talk about traditions around the world.

Lesson 11   Student's Book p. 108

✔ **Homework Check!**
Workbook p. 152, Activity 1 (Review)
Answers
1 Look and mark the statements T (True) or F (False). Correct the false statements.
1. T, 2. F; The eggs were boiled. 3. F; The meat was grilled. 4. F; The fish was baked. 5. T

Warm-up
Students play a game of *Go Fish* to review vocabulary.
- Students take out two pieces of paper and cut or tear them into 14 cards. On individual cards, they write the verbs *bake, roast, fry, steam, boil, grill*; on the rest they write the nouns *bread, meat, onion, dim sum, water, vegetables*.
- Students form groups of four. They combine and shuffle their cards.
- One student deals out five cards to each student and puts the rest in the center of the desk. This is the "pond."
- The student asks the student to the left of him / her for a card that matches one of the cards in his hand, for example, *boil*. If the student has a card that matches, for example *water* or *vegetables*, she gives it to him / her and he asks the student next to her for another card. If not, he / she says, "Go fish," and the student draws a card from the pile. If he draws a match, he continues play; if not, the play goes to the student on his left.
- Students play until all the words are matched up. The student with the most pairs wins.

1 Unscramble the words to complete the e-mail.
Students unscramble cooking vocabulary to complete the e-mail.
Answers
1. bakes, 2. roast, 3. raw, 4. fried, 5. boiled, 6. grilled, 7. steamed

2 Cross out the wrong word in each sentence.
Students identify the vocabulary word that does not make sense in each sentence.
Answers
1. grill, 2. boiled, 3. boil, 4. steamed, 5. Fried

3 Label the pictures with the words in the box.
Students identify the food adjective that goes with each picture.
Answers
top row spicy, crispy, bland, sticky, *bottom row* sour, raw, chewy

Wrap-up
Students race to brainstorm words to review vocabulary.
- Students form pairs.
- Say one of the adjectives to describe food from Activity 3 and set a stopwatch for one minute.
- Pairs write as many words as they can think of that the word describes until the stopwatch goes off.
- Continue saying the other words, setting the stopwatch for one minute each time.
- After you have said all seven words and students have had time to write for each, have students read them out loud.
- Students cross out words as they hear them.
- Once all words have been read aloud, the pair with the most words wins.

➡ **(No homework today.)**

 Teaching Tip
Keeping Teenage Students Interested
There is a specific challenge to teaching teens. Here are some tips for keeping them interested:
- Build rapport. This is essential for success. Showing a genuine interest in them and their lives will greatly improve your relationship with teens.
- Get to know their interests. Take time to get to know what they are interested in and use that in your lesson planning. You can do a survey at the beginning of the year and then use the results to inform your lessons.
- Build choice into your classroom activities. Obviously, you cannot just let students choose what they want to do, but once you have identified the objective of the class, you can offer a variety of ways of achieving it.
- Provide variety. Teens bore easily. Vary topics, types of tasks and ways of presenting material. Change the order in which you normally do things to breakdown classroom routine.
- Challenge your students. Create slightly more difficult tasks; introduce competition; go for open-ended tasks where appropriate.

Lesson 12   Student's Book p. 109

Warm-up
Students play a game called *Remember*. This to review the passive voice.
- Place five items, for example, a pencil, an eraser, a marker, a cell phone, a paper clip, etc., on a desk so that your students can see them clearly.
- Tell students to observe the placement of the items. Give them a minute or two to look.
- Tell students to close their eyes.
- Move the items on the desk to new places and / or add or replace other items.
- Students open their eyes and note the movement of the items using the passive voice, for example, *The paper clip was moved to the left. The ear buds were added.*
- Continue as long as time permits and students are engaged. You may ask volunteers to come up to the front of the class and make the changes to the items.

4 Write the correct number of response to each question.
Students match the statements and responses.

Answers
1. d, 2. c, 3. g, 4. a, 5. f, 6. e, 7. b

5 Write the correct number of sentence in each picture. Then change the sentences into the passive.
Students match the sentences to the photos and rewrite them in the passive.

Answers
3, 4, 5, 2, 1
1. Carnival is celebrated in Rio de Janeiro every year by Brazilians. 2. Thanksgiving is celebrated in the US and Canada in November. 3. A beautiful offering was made by Mexicans on last year's Day of the Dead. 4. The White Nights Festival is culminated by Russians with the Scarlet Sails celebration. 5. Last year, hundreds of people were injured by the running bulls in Pamplona.

Extension
Students play a game of *Jeopardy* to review.
- Draw the following chart on the board, or you may wish to project it:

Where is it?	Tastes	Cooking Verbs	Passive or Active
100	100	100	100
200	200	200	200
300	300	300	300
400	400	400	400

- Students form teams of four or five.
- Teams take turns choosing an amount and a category, for example, *Easter Island for 100.* You then ask them a question and if they answer correctly, that team gets a point.
- Play until all items have been covered and answered correctly. The team with the most points wins.
- Here are some items you can use:

Where Is It?
100: Maoris live in this country. (New Zealand)
200: The Tapati Festival is held here. (Easter Island)
300: Chicken and fish are not eaten on New Year's here. (the Philippines)
400: In this country, people eat bacon, fried eggs, sausages, and more for breakfast! (England)

Tastes
100: Baklava tastes like this. (sweet)
200: Goulash usually tastes like this. (spicy)
300: Rice, especially in Asia, often has this texture. (sticky)
400: This is what a lemon taste like. (sour)

Cooking Verbs
100: This is when bread or a pie is cooked in the oven. (baked)
200: This is when water or rice is cooked on the stove over a very high heat. (boiled)
300: This is when meat or vegetables are cooked in the oven. (roasted)
400: This is when something is cooked in oil or butter on the stove. (fried)

Passive or Active?
100: Hungarians eat a lot of spicy food. (active)
200: Ceviche is prepared with lemons or limes. (passive)
300: The tandoori chicken was delicious. (active)
400: Noodles are eaten all over Asia. (passive)

Big Question
Students are given the opportunity to revisit the Big Question and reflect on it.
- Ask students to turn to the unit opener on page 97 and think about the question *What's it like in your country?*
- Ask students to think about what the have learned about other places and traditions, the readings they've read, the texts they've listened to and the recipe they came up with.
- Students form small groups to discuss the following:
  » *What impression do you think visitors to your country have?*
  » *Is food important to culture? Explain.*
  » *Do you think it's important to try new things, including food, when you go to a new place? Why or why not?*
- Monitor, offering help as needed, particularly with vocabulary.

Scorecard
Hand out (and/or project) a *Scorecard*. Have students fill in their *Scorecards* for this unit.

▸ **Study for the unit test.**

8 What's your dream job?

Grammar	Vocabulary
Defining Clauses: A paleontologist is a scientist <u>who investigates fossils</u>. **Non-defining Clauses:** Formula 1 drivers, <u>who come from many different countries,</u> risk their lives every time they are in a race. **Relative Pronouns:** *that, which, who*	**Unusual Jobs:** animation director, chef, sports coach, computer game programmer, crime scene investigator, graffiti artist, marine biologist, travel writer

Reading	Writing
Previewing to predict content	Writing a summary

In the first lesson, read the unit title aloud and have students look carefully at the unit cover. Encourage them to think about the message in the picture. At the end of the unit, students will discuss the big question: *What's your dream job?*

 **Teaching Tip**

Reflecting on Your Teaching

Take time to critically reflect on your teaching. Consider the following questions:
- What were my goals for this class? Did I achieve them?
- Which lessons were the most effective? Which were the least effective?
- Which activities did the students respond to best? Why do you think this was so?
- What did I learn from this class?

Reflecting on your teaching, not only at the end of a course, but throughout contributes to higher-quality teaching. Keeping a diary or making notes after each class is a good way to reflect on your classroom practices regularly.

Objective
Students will be able to understand and use **unusual jobs** vocabulary.

Lesson 1   Student's Book pp. 112 and 113

Warm-up

Students brainstorm and rank jobs to generate interest and activate prior knowledge.
- Write the word *JOBS* on the board and set a stopwatch for one minute.
- Students form groups of three and brainstorm as many jobs as they can until the stopwatch goes off.
- Have groups rank their jobs in order of preference.
- When students have finished, come together as a class and have students share their lists and rankings.

1 Work in small groups and discuss the questions.

Students discuss the questions about jobs in small groups.

2 Read the introduction to a podcast. Then label the pictures with the jobs in the box.

Students read the "Dream Jobs" text for context and match the vocabulary words with the photos.

Answers

a. chef, b. crime scene investigator, c. animation director, d. marine biologist, e. travel writer, f. sports coach, g. graffiti artist, h. computer game programmer

114

3 🎧 39 Listen and number the pictures in Activity 2 in the order you hear them.

Students listen to the podcast and match the speakers to the jobs.

Answers

a. 4, b. 8, c. 5, d. 7, e. 1, f. 3, g. 2, h. 6

Audio Script

1. I'm very lucky to have my dream job. I go all around the world and write about my experiences. I'm a travel writer. I got this job because of my languages. I speak Spanish and English. I also have the right qualifications—I have a degree in Journalism.
2. I'm a graffiti artist. It's an amazing job. I paint walls, doors and other things for companies. I have a contract to paint an advertising campaign. It's going to be so cool.
3. Actually, my dream job was to be a pro ice skater. Unfortunately, I had to retire after I broke my leg very badly. Now I'm an ice skating coach and I train kids in speed skating. It's fun.
4. My grandma taught me to cook and I always dreamed of becoming a chef. The only bad thing about my job is the long hours. We work evenings and weekends. We live our whole lives in the kitchen.
5. I work in animated movies. I studied character animation and today I'm an animation director. I manage a team of artists and I tell them what to do. I have a very creative job!
6. I always loved computer games. I play them all the time. So when I saw the job advertisement for a computer game programmer, I decided to apply for it. I got it and now I love my job. I design games and play them all day. It's bliss.
7. I'm not interested in money. I care about the environment. I'm a scientist, a marine biologist and I work with sharks. Working with animals is a dream. I really feel like I make a difference.
8. I grew up reading crime fiction—Sherlock Holmes, Agatha Christie—and I always wanted to be a detective. In fact, I'm a crime scene investigator. It's my dream job, but we see some terrible things and we deal with many different problems.

Stop and Think! Critical Thinking

How is talent related to the job that someone chooses to do?
- Have students meet with their classmates from the Warm-up and take out their lists.
- Ask *What skills are needed to do those jobs?*
- Students discuss for a few minutes.
- Then ask *How is talent related to the job that someone chooses to do?*
- Students discuss in their groups and then as a class.

Extension
Students do a word puzzle to practice job vocabulary.
- Make a word search online goo.gl/32r7RW or a crossword goo.gl/fQ7Chh.
- Have students do the puzzle in class or at home.
- Be sure to go over the answers.

Wrap-up

Students play a game of *Charades* to review job vocabulary.
- Students form groups of four.
- They take turns acting out the jobs from Activity 2, while their group mates try to guess what they are.

➧ **Workbook p. 154, Activities 1 and 2**

Lesson 2 — Student's Book pp. 112 and 113

> ✔ **Homework Check!**
> Workbook p. 154, Activities 1 and 2
>
> **Answers**
> **1 Look and write the jobs.**
> 1. computer game programmer, 2. marine biologist, 3. chef, 4. travel writer
> **2 Read and write the jobs.**
> 1. crime scene investigator, 2. animation director, 3. graffiti artist, 4. marine biologist, 5. travel writer, 6. computer game programmer, 7. chef

Warm-up

Students play a game of *Pictionary* to review job vocabulary.
- Students form groups of three or four.
- Set a stopwatch for three minutes.
- A student from each groups draws one of the jobs from the vocabulary. He / She is not allowed to speak or write words, only draw pictures.
- Once a student guesses the phrase, another student from the group draws pictures to represent another phrase.
- When the stopwatch goes off, the group with the most correctly guessed vocabulary items wins.

4 🎧³⁹ **Complete the sentences with the words in the box. Then listen again and check.**

Students complete the excerpts from the listening with words from the box and listen again to check their answers.

Answers

1. qualifications, 2. contract, 3. retire, 4. long, 5. manage, 6. apply, 7. make, 8. deal

5 Complete the table with jobs from Activity 2. Add more jobs.

Students categorize jobs vocabulary according to their endings and add more jobs they know to each one.

Answers

-ant Answers will vary. *-er* computer game programmer, travel writer, *-or* crime scene investigator, animation director, *-ist* graffiti artist, marine biologist, *other* chef

6 Think Fast! Think of one more job…

Students do a three-minute timed challenge: they think of additional jobs that fit each description.

Answers

Answers will vary.

7 Look at the jobs on both pages and complete the table below. Then compare it with a partner.

In a personalization activity, students complete the table according to their opinions and thoughts about the different jobs.

Answers

Answers will vary.

Wrap-up

Students play a game of *Twenty Questions* to review job vocabulary and verbs.
- Students take out a piece of paper and cut or tear it into eight pieces. They write one of the jobs from Activity 2 on each piece of paper. (Note: If you have covered more jobs than those in Activity 2, have students add these cards to the deck.)
- Students form groups of three or four.
- They shuffle their decks of cards and then, without looking, choose one.
- Students ask the first student *yes/no* questions to find out the job. They may ask 20 questions in total.
- The student who guesses the job correctly gets a point. If students cannot guess the job, the student being asked questions gets a point.
- Students play until all the jobs have been found out.
- The student with the most points wins.

➡ **Workbook pp. 154 and 155, Activities 3 and 4**

Objectives
Students will be able to use **defining** and **non-defining relative clauses** to describe jobs.

Lesson 3   Student's Book p. 114

> ✔ **Homework Check!**
> Workbook pp. 154 and 155, Activities 3 and 4
> **Answers**
> **3 Match the words to their definitions.**
> 1. c, 2. b, 3. a, 4. d, 5. g, 6. f
> **4 Choose words from Activity 3 and fill in the mind maps below. Add more words if necessary.**
> Answers will vary.

Warm-up
Students play a word game to review job vocabulary.
- Write the word *JOBS* on the board and underline the letter *J*.
- Students form pairs.
- Set a stopwatch for one minute. Pairs write as many jobs as they can think of that begin with the letter J.
- Continue with the other letters, one minute for each.
- When the final stopwatch goes off, the pair with the most words wins.

1 Read the descriptions of each job. Then write the correct number of description in each picture.
Students are exposed to relative clauses as they read the descriptions and match them to the pictures.
Answers
1. c, 2. e, 3. a, 4. f, 5. b, 6. d

2 Look again at the sentences in Activity 1 and follow the instructions.
Students identify the relative clauses in the previous activity and determine whether each one is defining or non-defining.
- Draw students' attention to the **Defining and Non-defining Relative Clauses** box and read the information aloud. Explain non-defining clauses provide extra information and are between commas.

Answers
Defining who studies fossils, which features the world's fastest cars, who plays music in nightclubs, who writes guidebooks, who cuts the hair of animals, that help people to relax; *Non-defining* which was found in Argentina, who come from many different countries, which means "disk jockey", which comes from Australia, which have very long hair, which comes from India

3 Replace *that* in the defining relative clauses with *who* or *which*. Write the relative pronouns on the lines.
Students determine whether *who* or *which* should be used in each sentence.
Answers
1. who, 2. which, 3. which, 4. which, 5. who, 6. who

Extension
Students write a *Chain Story* to practice relative clauses.
- Students form groups of five.
- Each student takes out a piece of paper and writes at the top *It was the day that …* and completes it with his own idea.
- They fold the paper over so that the sentence cannot be seen and passes it to the student next to him.
- That student completes this sentence: *There was a girl / boy who …* They fold over the top and pass it to the next student.
- That student finishes this sentence: *She / He met a girl / boy who …*
- When the fourth student gets the paper, he finishes this sentence: *They had to fight against a monster that …*
- The fifth and final student finishes this sentence: *The ending was something that …*
- When all five students have finished their sentences, have them read their stories to each other.
- Have a few students read some of their groups' stories aloud to the class.

Wrap-up
Students play a guessing game to review jobs vocabulary and relative clauses.
- Write the following phrase on the board: *I like a job that …*
- Model by saying a few sentences about your dream job, for example, *I like a job that lets me work with people.*
- Continue saying other sentences, using relative clauses until your students guess and say *Your dream job is being a teacher.*
- Students form groups of three or four. They take turns saying sentences about their dream jobs, while other students try to guess what they are.

▶ **Workbook p. 155, Activities 1 and 2**

Lesson 4
Student's Book p. 115

> ✔ **Homework Check!**
> Workbook p. 155, Activities 1 and 2
> **Answers**
> **1 Read the relative clauses and write *D* (Defining) or *ND* (Non-defining).**
> 1. ND, 2. D, 3. D, 4. D, 5. ND
> **2 Rewrite the sentences using relative clauses. Include commas where necessary.**
> 1. A botanist is a type of scientist who / that studies plants. 2. My dad, who is very competitive, won employee of the month. 3. Mr. Kelly, who is is from France, is the school principal.
> 4. Engineers, who are in-demand, design materials, structures and systems. 5. The career of speech pathology, which is a growing field, deals with communication disorders.

Warm-up
Students play a game of *Memory* to practice relative clauses.
- Have students take out a piece of paper and tear it into four long horizontal pieces. They fold each piece in half vertically.
- On one side of each piece of paper, students write the beginning of a sentence, and on the other side, they write an appropriate relative clause to complete the sentence.
- Students then tear the sentences in half.
- Students form pairs and shuffle both sets of cards.
- They spread the cards out, face-down, between them.
- Students take turns turning over two cards, trying to match the two parts of the sentences. If a student makes a match, he / she keeps the cards and continues. If not, he / she turns the cards back to their original place and the play goes to the other student.
- Students play until all cards are matched. The student with the most cards wins.

4 Rewrite the sentences to include the extra information. Write the extra information between commas.
Students combine two sentences into one using non-defining relative clauses.

Answers
1. Bikram, which is my favorite type of yoga, is done in a sauna-like room. 2. My sister, who is 21, works as a paleontologist. 3. Orthodontists, who are very well paid, help straighten your teeth. 4. J. K. Rowling, who is British, is the author of the Harry Potter books. 5. Mr. Clements, who teaches us drama, will be the director of the school play.

5 Cross out six relative pronouns that can be omitted in the article.
Students identify the relative pronouns in the article that are not necessary.

- Draw students' attention to the **Defining Relative Clauses** box and read the information aloud, focusing on the explanation of when relative pronouns can be omitted.

Answers
1. who I know, 2. which they hate, 3. which they are going to describe, 4. who I often ask,
5. that tourists never find, 6. that you have never met before

6 Follow the instructions and play the game with a partner.
Students follow the steps to play a game practicing relative clauses in pairs. Encourage them to be creative writing their definitions.

Wrap-up
Students play a game of *Apples to Apples* to practice relative clauses.
- Have students take out a piece of paper and tear it into 10 pieces. Ask them to write a job or a word related to a job on each card.
- Students form groups of four or five and shuffle their cards together.
- One student deals five cards to each person.
- The student to the left of the dealer lays one card face up on the desk.
- The other students must then choose one of their cards that they think best connects with the one on the desk.
- Once everyone has laid down their card, students take turns explaining the connection between their cards using relative clauses.
- The student who laid the card on the table decides which student's connection he likes best, and that student gets a point.
- Continue playing until everyone has had a chance to lay the first card in a round or until one of the players scores five points.

Workbook p. 156, Activities 3 and 4

> **Teaching Tip**
> **Asking Deductive Questions for Concept Checking**
> Check for comprehension by asking students deductive questions closely related to the target concept. For example, if you are working on relative clauses like this: *Jim is the paleontologist who found those fossils.* Check if students understand the difference between a defining clause and non-defining clause by asking *If we take away the clause "who found those fossils," does the sentence make sense?* Elicit *No*, and then explain that defining clauses are necessary to understanding what or who the noun is.

 **Reading & Writing**

Objectives
Students will be able to preview to **predict content** in a magazine article about the job of an artist. They will also be able to **write a summary**.

Lesson 5 Student's Book pp. 116 and 117

> ✔ Homework Check!
> Workbook p. 156, Activities 3 and 4
> Answers
> **3 Correct one mistake in each sentence and rewrite it.**
> 1. A school counselor is a <u>person who</u> gives advice about career opportunities. 2. An interpreter, <u>which</u> is a great career for bilinguals, involves spoken language. 3. Human resources professionals are specialists <u>who</u> help companies find qualified employees. 4. My <u>dream, which</u> is to be an <u>actor, is</u> a difficult one to achieve. 5. Accountants are <u>people who</u> prepare and examine financial records.
> **4 Read the defining relative clauses and write S (Subject relative clause) or O (Object relative clause). Cross out the relative pronouns that can be omitted.**
> 1. O, ~~that~~, 2. S, 3. O, ~~who~~, 4. O, ~~that~~, 5. O, ~~which~~, 6. S

▶ 118 **Warm-up**
Students discuss what they see in photos.
- Show students the photos on pages 116 and 117.
- Ask *What can you see?* Elicit responses. If necessary, point out the figure of the man in the photos.
- Ask *Why do you think the artist created his pictures like this?*
- Students form groups of three to discuss.
- Monitor, offering help as needed.
- Come together as a class and have some students share their thoughts and ideas.

1 Complete the article with the letters of the missing sentences.
Students determine where the sentences fit best in the article.
Answers
1. e, 2. g, 3. d, 4. b, 5. f, 6. a, 7. c

2 Circle T (True) or F (False).
Students answer true/false comprehension questions about the article.
Answers
1. F, 2. F, 3. T, 4. F, 5. F, 6. T

3 Read the definition of a summary in the *Be Strategic!* section. Then underline useful key words to remember.
Students read the information in the *Be Strategic* box and identify key words that will help them remember how to create a summary.
Answers
Answers will vary.

4 Read the examples of sentences from a summary and underline the verbs used in each one.
Students identify verbs often used in summaries in the example sentences.
Answers
argues, shows, states, reveals

Stop and Think! Critical Thinking
How does Liu Bolin express passion for what he does? Does he convey a message through his work?
- Remind students of their discussion in the Warm-up.
- Ask *How does Liu Bolin express passion for what he does?* Draw students' attention to the text, encouraging them to find evidence.
- Then ask *Does he convey a message through his work? If so, what?*
- Students form pairs to discuss.

> **Extension**
> Students conduct research on an artist.
> - Draw students' attention to the photos on pages 116 and 117.
> - Ask *Do you like Liu Bolin's photos?* Elicit some answers.
> - Have students choose or assign an artist for students, or groups of students, to research.
> - Students present their findings to the class.

Wrap-up
Students retell the text with a swapping activity.
- Students write down the key words they underlined in the Activity 3.
- They form pairs and swap papers.
- Students take turns retelling the text, using their partner's text.
- Monitor, offering help as needed.

▶ **Workbook p. 157, Activities 1 and 2**

Lesson 6 — Student's Book pp. 116 and 117

> ✔ **Homework Check!**
> Workbook p. 157, Activities 1 and 2
>
> **Answers**
> **1 Read the article and mark (✓) the health care career you prefer.**
> Answers will vary.
> **2 Answer the following questions.**
> 1. There is a growing population of older people.
> 2. Job security, flexibility, they are in demand.
> 3. Training after high school, college degree, postgraduate studies.

Warm-up
Students retell a text with prompts.
- Draw students' attention to the sentences in Activity 1.
- Students form pairs and take turns retelling the text, using only the sentences as prompts.
- Monitor, offering help as needed.

5 🎧⁴⁰ **Number the sentences to complete a summary of Liu Bolin's article. Then listen and check.**
Students put the sentences in order to form a summary of the article about Liu Bolin. They listen to the audio to check their answers.

Answers
2, 6, 4, 7, 8, 1, 5, 3

Audio Script
This article discusses the work of Chinese artist Liu Bolin. Liu Bolin makes photographs where he disappears into the background. The author, Roberta Ward, argues that these photos show how people feel in modern cities. According to Liu Bolin, people feel small in today's cities, as if they are invisible. Ward also explains how Liu makes his photos. He works with a team of makeup artists and photographers to create the final image. These people work for about 10 hours on each image. Finally, Ward reveals that Liu is preparing new projects which will look at the Internet.

6 **Think Fast! Name as many artists as you know. They can be from the past, too.**
Students do a two-minute timed challenge: they list as many artists as they can think of.

Answers
Answers will vary.

7 Now write a summary of a text from another unit. Follow the steps.
Students use the steps as a guideline for writing their own summaries of another text they choose from their Student's Book. If possible, mark their summaries and provide each student feedback on grammar, spelling and punctuation.

Answers
Answers will vary.

Extension
Students hold an art exhibition to personalize the lesson.
- Students brainstorm different art media, for example, *photography, painting (watercolors, tempera, oil, etc.), drawing (pencil, charcoal, crayon, etc.), collage, sculpture.*
- Ask students to bring in some of their art. Encourage them to bring in something without worrying about "quality."
- Display the art around your classroom.
- Have each artist explain their piece to the class.

Wrap-up
Students share their summaries and try to guess the text.
- Students form pairs.
- They read their summaries aloud to each other, while their partner tries to locate the text in the Student's Book.
- Monitor, offering help as needed.

➡ **Workbook p. 157, Activity 3**

Preparing for the Next Lesson
Ask students to watch an introduction to king crab fishing in Alaska: goo.gl/iBNd6G or invite them to look around on the web site: goo.gl/q1HBJN.

 Culture

Objective
Students will be able to use **relative clauses** to talk about a dangerous job in Alaska.

Lesson 7   Student's Book p. 118 and 119

> ✔ **Homework Check!**
> Workbook p. 157, Activity 3
> **Answers**
> **3 In your notebook, write a paragraph about your dream job.**
> Answers will vary.

Warm-up
Students make a KWL Chart to preview the topic.
• Draw a KWL Chart on the board, similar to following:

What I Know	What I Want to Know	What I Have Learned

• Ask students to write about what they know about Alaska and what they want to know.
• Tell students that they will read about Alaska.

 120

1 🎧⁴¹ **Circle the correct options to complete the text. Then listen and check.**
Students guess the facts about Alaska and listen to the audio to check their answers.

Answers
1. biggest, 2. Juneau, 3. sea, 4. Russia, 5. Five, 6. most

Audio Script
Alaska is the biggest state in the US. The capital is Juneau. The name Alaska means "that which the sea breaks against." The US purchased Alaska from Russia in 1867. Alaska's native population include Eskimos, Indians and Aleuts. Five percent of the state is covered by glaciers. If you ever go to Alaska, you might be lucky enough to watch one crash into the ocean. The Bering Sea is one of the world's most productive fishing grounds, producing huge quantities of king crab, salmon and other varieties of fish.

2 Discuss the questions with a partner.
To encourage interest in the topic, students discuss the questions about king crab fishing in pairs.

3 Label the text with the correct headings in the box.
Students read the text and determine which heading best fits each paragraph.
• Draw students' attention to the **Guess What!** box. Tell them that the Discovery Channel started a documentary-style show in 2005 that shows the drama behind the crabbing industry in Alaska. It's called *Deadliest Catch* and it has 12 seasons!
• Have students read the text and write the correct headings.
• Check answers as a class.

Answers
1. Fishing, 2. Boats, 3. Crabs, 4. Hazards

Stop and Think! Value
Is it worth risking your life for a job that pays well?
• Ask *Do you think the job of a king crabber pays well?* Ask students to estimate a crabber's salary and tell them they will read more about their salary in the next lesson.
• Then ask *Is it worth risking your life for a job that pays well? Explain*.
• Students form pairs to discuss.

Wrap-up
Students complete their KWL Charts.
• Students take out their KWL Charts from the Warm-up and complete the final column.
• Students form small groups of three or four and share what they have learned.
• Encourage students to discuss some of the following questions:
  » *What was the most interesting thing you learned?*
  » *What was the most surprising thing you learned?*
  » *Would you like to go to Alaska? Why or why not?*
  » *Why do you think some people are attracted to dangerous jobs?*
• Monitor, offering help as needed.
• Come together as a class and have some students share their thoughts and ideas.

➡ **(No homework today.)**

 Teaching Tip
Scanning the Text First
Before your students read, have them scan the text first. Scanning is when you read to get the gist, or general idea, of a text before reading again for more detail. Demonstrate how to scan by putting the text up on a projector or whiteboard if possible. Point out the title and headings to give them a clue to what the text is about.

Lesson 8   Student's Book p. 119

Warm-up

Students play a game of *Hangman* to review vocabulary.

- Draw a hangman's gallows, like this, on the board:

- Choose one of the glossary words or words from the text, for example, *treacherous*, and write the same number of blanks as there are letters in the word on the board:

—— —— —— —— —— —— —— —— —— ——

- Students form two or three teams. Team members take turns calling out letters. If a student calls out a letter that is part of the word, for example, *t*, write that letter in the appropriate blank or blanks. If it is not part of the word, draw the person on the gallows, beginning with the head. Draw one part of the body for each letter called that is not part of the word. Be sure to write the called-out letter to the side of the gallows so that students don't call it out again.
- The game is over when teams have either guessed the word, completed the word, or the body is complete.
- If time permits, have a student come up to the board and choose a word, while others call out letters and try to guess it. Award points for correct guesses.

4 Write the correct letter of the missing clauses.

Students identify which sentence each relative clause fits in.

Answers

1. c, 2. d, 3. a, 4. e, 5. b

5 Read the job ad. In your notebook, make a list of the pros and cons.

Students read the ad for a king crabbing position and list the pros and cons of the job. Ask them if their estimate of a crabber's salary in the last lesson was close to the one in the ad. Ask them if they would apply for the job. Discuss as a class.

Answers

Answers will vary.

Extension

Students write and respond to a job ad to consolidate the lesson.

- Draw students' attention to the job ad in Activity 5.
- Students form pairs and choose another job from the unit.
- They write a job ad with similar criteria.
- Monitor, offering help as needed.
- Collect the ads and then redistribute them to new pairs.
- Pairs make a list of the pros and cons of the job.
- Have some pairs share their ideas.

Wrap-up

Students play a game of *Taboo* to review the text.

- Write one of the words from the text on the board, for example, *deck*. Underline the word and write these words under it: *ship, stand, hands*.
- Place a chair in front of the class with the board behind it. This is the "hot seat."
- Model the activity by sitting in the hot seat. Explain to students that they should describe the word *deck* without saying the word, or any forms of the word, or saying the words *ship, stand, hands*. These words are "taboo."
- Divide the class into three or four teams. Place additional chairs in front of the class, as many as there are teams. Choose one member from each team to sit in the hot seats.
- Write another word and taboo words on the board. Here are some ideas:
  » bait: crabs, set, traps
  » pots: container, catch, store
  » sardines: fish, catch, ocean
  » treacherous: dangerous, difficult, deal with
  » competition: race, test, friendship
  » drown: die, underwater, breathe
  » life-threatening: danger, accident, scary
- Each team appoints one team member to describe the word, without saying the taboo words, to their team member.
- Set a stopwatch for fifteen seconds. Each team has fifteen seconds to describe the word.
- The team that guesses correctly gets a point.
- New members come up to sit in the hot seats. Then write another word and taboo words on the board and set the stopwatch.
- Follow the same procedure until all words have been reviewed. The team with the most points wins.

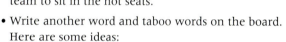 **(No homework today.)**

Objective
Students will be able to use **relative clauses** to organize a tribe.

Lesson 9 Student's Book p. 120

Warm-up
Students play a game called *Two Truths and a Lie* to generate interest and activate prior knowledge.
- Say three statements about your abilities, but two are true and one is a lie. For example, say *I can carry 80 kilograms. I am a very talented actor. I am very handy and can fix anything.*
- Students form pairs and decide which two are true and which one is a lie.
- Students think of three statements about themselves, two that are true and one that is a lie.
- Students form groups of three or four and say their statements. The others try to guess which is the lie.

1 Complete the survey about you.
Students complete a survey about their preferences and abilities.

Answers
Answers will vary.

2 Work in groups. Compare your answers to Activity 1 and discuss the questions.
Students form their project groups and discuss their survey results.

3 In groups, read the situation and discuss the questions.
Students read the scenario about the disaster on Earth for the organization of their tribes and begin to make plans.

Extension
Students play a game called *Shipwrecked* to build on the lesson.
- Draw a picture on the board of an island and a sinking ship or bring one in to show your students.
- Students form groups of four or five.
- Tell students that they have been shipwrecked on a deserted island. They must try to survive.
- Write the following questions on the board:
  » *What eight items (and only eight) will you bring?*
  » *What possible problems will you encounter?*
  » *How will you solve them?*
  » *How will you make decisions?*
  » *Who will be your leader?*
  » *What sort of laws will you have in place?*
  » *How will you punish those who break the laws?*
- Groups discuss the questions.
- Monitor, offering help as needed.
- Have students share their answers with the class. Challenge students to share their rationale for their choices.

Wrap-up
Students brainstorm potential problems to consolidate the lesson and prepare for the next activity.
- Students meet with their groups.
- Draw their attention to the situation in Activity 3.
- Ask *What are some potential problems that might arise?*
- Students discuss and brainstorm potential problems.
- Monitor, offering help as needed. Encourage them to think of possible solutions to the problems.
- Come together as a class and have some students share their thoughts and ideas.

Lesson 10 Student's Book p. 121

Warm-up

Students play a game called *Last Man Standing* to generate interest and activate prior knowledge.

- Remind students they are still in their tribes. Ask *What will you do to contribute to your tribe?*
- The first student makes a sentence, stating what he'll / she'll do for his / her tribe.
- The student next to him / her says what that student will do and makes a statement about himself / herself.
- The student next to him / her must say what the previous students will do, as well as what he / she will do.
- If a student can't remember what the others have said, he / she sits down and is out of the game.
- Continue until there is only one student left standing. That student wins.

Stop and Think! Critical Thinking

Is there a possibility nowadays to cause the extinction of humankind? What could cause it?

- Read the *Stop and Think!* box aloud and ask students to share their ideas.
- Elicit a few causes of human extinction. Encourage students to discuss the causes that are responsibility of humans.
- After a few minutes, bring the class together and discuss their ideas.
- Ask students how we can prevent a disaster on Earth and discuss as a class.
- After a few minutes, bring the class together and discuss their ideas.

4 **Now, you will get ready to assign jobs in your tribe. First, look at the jobs below and rank them from 1 (most important) to 8 (least important).**
Students rank the jobs in order of importance in the context of a disaster on Earth.

5 **Assign jobs in your tribe. Follow the steps.**
Students organize themselves in their tribes and determine which jobs each member will be responsible for.

6 **In groups, discuss the questions.**
Students discuss the questions listed to reflect on how they organized their tribes and the possible threats.

Wrap-up

Students role-play the situation to consolidate the lesson.

- Students meet in their groups.
- They go over the roles they were assigned.
- Tell students that they will act out the first day after the disaster.
- Students spend some time thinking about what they need to fulfill their roles.

- Monitor, offering help as needed.
- Students practice their role-plays and if time allows, perform them for the class.

▶ **Workbook p. 156, Activity 1 (Review)**

> **Teaching Tip**
>
> **Incorporating Role-plays into the Classroom**
> Role-plays add variety, a change of pace and opportunities for authentic language practice, not to mention they can be a lot of fun. Also role-plays give all students, especially quieter ones, a chance to express themselves. Rather than simply using a written dialogue or text, encourage students to be creative and "take on" their roles. Give students enough time to practice, but discourage them from learning their parts by heart. Allow them to use props to reflect a real-life situation when possible. Your role in role-plays is three-fold: facilitator (you may need to offer support, particularly with new language), spectator (you watch and offer feedback at the end) and participant (sometimes it's appropriate to get involved and take part in the role-play yourself). The most important component to any successful role-play is to keep it real and relevant to students.

Review

Objectives
Students will be able to use **unusual jobs** vocabulary as well as **defining** and **non-defining relative clauses**.

Lesson 11   Student's Book p. 122

> ✔ **Homework Check!**
> Workbook p. 156, Activity 1 (Review)
> **Answers**
> 1 Complete the job descriptions using relative clauses.
> Answers will vary.

Warm-up

Students have a spelling bee to review job vocabulary.
- Students form two to three groups and line up in front of the board.
- Give the first student in each group a marker.
- Say one of the jobs from the unit. Each student writes the word on the board without looking at the other students.
- If a student spells the word correctly, the group gets a point.
- The students pass the markers to the next students in line. Say another job for those students to spell.
- Continue until you have reviewed all the vocabulary.
- The group with the most correctly spelled words wins.
- Challenge students to use the words in sentences or to define them, awarding points for correct usage and definitions.

1 Number the pictures that are related to each job below.
Students identify the unusual jobs vocabulary words that are represented by each photo.
Answers
1st row 2, *2nd row* 4, 6, *3rd row* 1, 8, *4th row* 5, 3, 7

2 Complete the dialogues with the jobs in Activity 1.
Students practice using the unusual jobs vocabulary in context.
Answers
1. sports coach, 2. marine biologist, 3. animation director, 4. chef, 5. computer game programmer, 6. travel writer, 7. graffiti artist, 8. crime scene investigator

Wrap-up

Students play a game of *What's My Line?* to review vocabulary.
- Students take out one or two pieces of paper and tear them into cards.
- They write a job on each, looking back through the Student's Book and their notes.
- Students form groups of three or four.
- They shuffle their cards and place them in a pile, face-down, in front of them.
- The first student turns over a card, but doesn't show it to his / her group mates.
- He / She starts to describe the job as if it were his / her job: *I work with people, but they aren't alive. I work all over the city …*
- The first student to guess the job says it aloud. If the student is correct, he takes the card and then describes one from his deck. If not, the first student continues to describe the job.
- Students play as time permits or until all jobs have been described.
- The student with most cards in his group wins.

 (No homework today.)

> 🐝 **Teaching Tip**
> **Making Use of Pop Culture in the Classroom**
> Be open to discussing the latest trends with your students. Use it as a springboard for classroom activities. However, here are some words of caution:
> - Don't be the one to choose. Chances are, what you think is currently trending isn't any more. Let your students lead the way with topics and trends.
> - Don't act as if you enjoy the things they like if you don't. Allowing for them to discuss their interests doesn't mean you have to share them. Plus, they can spot when you're being false.
> - Keep up with the times. Just because your students liked something last year doesn't mean this year's class will have the same response. Consider this when you invest time and energy into making teaching materials.

Lesson 12   Student's Book p. 123

Warm-up

Students play a game of *Clues* to review relative clauses.
- Students form two groups.
- Groups take turns choosing an object in the room to give clues about. Each clue must start with *This is something that / which …*
- Each team gives three clues for its chosen object.
- If the other team is able to guess the object after just one clue, award them three points. If they need two clues, award them two points. If they need three, award them one point. If unable to guess the object, they get no points.
- Play until one team scores 12 points.

3 Complete the missing letters.

Students write the letters to spell the words related to jobs.

Answers

1. long, 2. retire, 3. contract, 4. earn, 5. qualifications, 6. apply, 7. manages, 8. deal

4 Complete the text with *who* or *which*.

Students determine which relative pronoun should be used in each clause.

Answers

1. who, 2. who, 3. which, 4. who, 5. who, 6. which, 7. which, 8. who, 9. which, 10. which

5 Add commas around the non-defining relative clauses. Mark (✓) the correct sentences.

Students determine which relative clauses are non-defining and require commas.

Answers

1. ✓, 2. … mom, who works for the police, is; 3. curry, which comes; 4. coach, who we really like, is; 5. programmer, which is

Extension

Students put together scrambled sentences to practice relative clauses.
- Write several sentences using relative clauses. Make as many sets as there are groups of three in your class.
- Cut apart the sentences into three pieces—the beginning of the sentences, the relative clauses and the end of the sentences.
- Shuffle all the pieces of a set together and give them to a group of three students.
- Students reassemble the sentences.
- The group that finishes first, with all sentences correct wins.

Big Question

Students are given the opportunity to revisit the Big Question and reflect on it.
- Ask students to turn to the unit opener on page 111 and think about the question *What's your dream job?*
- Ask students to think about the discussions they've had on jobs, the readings they've read, the map they read and role-play they did.
- Students form small groups to discuss the following:
  » *How important is your salary?*
  » *Would you take a job that didn't pay well but was interesting?*
  » *Would you relocate for your job?*
  » *What is your dream job?*
- Monitor, offering help as needed, particularly with vocabulary.

⭐ Scorecard

Hand out (and/or project) a *Scorecard*. Have students fill in their *Scorecards* for this unit.

➡ **Study for the unit test.**

CD1 and CD2 Contents

CD 1

Worksheets

- **Grammar Worksheets**
  - Stopwatch 5 Grammar Answer Key.pdf
  - Stopwatch 5 Unit 0 Grammar 1 (5.0.G1).pdf
  - Stopwatch 5 Unit 0 Grammar 2 (5.0.G2).pdf
  - Stopwatch 5 Unit 1 Grammar 1 (5.1.G1).pdf
  - Stopwatch 5 Unit 1 Grammar 2 (5.1.G2).pdf
  - Stopwatch 5 Unit 2 Grammar 1 (5.2.G1).pdf
  - Stopwatch 5 Unit 2 Grammar 2 (5.2.G2).pdf
  - Stopwatch 5 Unit 3 Grammar 1 (5.3.G1).pdf
  - Stopwatch 5 Unit 3 Grammar 2 (5.3.G2).pdf
  - Stopwatch 5 Unit 4 Grammar 1 (5.4.G1).pdf
  - Stopwatch 5 Unit 4 Grammar 2 (5.4.G2).pdf
  - Stopwatch 5 Unit 5 Grammar 1 (5.5.G1).pdf
  - Stopwatch 5 Unit 5 Grammar 2 (5.5.G2).pdf
  - Stopwatch 5 Unit 6 Grammar 1 (5.6.G1).pdf
  - Stopwatch 5 Unit 6 Grammar 2 (5.6.G2).pdf
  - Stopwatch 5 Unit 7 Grammar 1 (5.7.G1).pdf
  - Stopwatch 5 Unit 7 Grammar 2 (5.7.G2).pdf
  - Stopwatch 5 Unit 8 Grammar 1 (5.8.G1).pdf
  - Stopwatch 5 Unit 8 Grammar 2 (5.8.G2).pdf
- **Reading Worksheets**
  - Stopwatch 5 Answer Key Reading.pdf
  - Stopwatch 5 Unit 1 Reading 1 (5.1.R1).pdf
  - Stopwatch 5 Unit 1 Reading 2 (5.1.R2).pdf
  - Stopwatch 5 Unit 2 Reading 1 (5.2.R1).pdf
  - Stopwatch 5 Unit 2 Reading 2 (5.2.R2).pdf
  - Stopwatch 5 Unit 3 Reading 1 (5.3.R1).pdf
  - Stopwatch 5 Unit 3 Reading 2 (5.3.R2).pdf
  - Stopwatch 5 Unit 4 Reading 1 (5.4.R1).pdf
  - Stopwatch 5 Unit 4 Reading 2 (5.4.R2).pdf
  - Stopwatch 5 Unit 5 Reading 1 (5.5.R1).pdf
  - Stopwatch 5 Unit 5 Reading 2 (5.5.R2).pdf
  - Stopwatch 5 Unit 6 Reading 1 (5.6.R1).pdf
  - Stopwatch 5 Unit 6 Reading 2 (5.6.R2).pdf
  - Stopwatch 5 Unit 7 Reading 1 (5.7.R1).pdf
  - Stopwatch 5 Unit 7 Reading 2 (5.7.R2).pdf
  - Stopwatch 5 Unit 8 Reading 1 (5.8.R1).pdf
  - Stopwatch 5 Unit 8 Reading 2 (5.8.R2).pdf
  - Stopwatch Reading Worksheets Guidelines.pdf
- **Vocabulary Worksheets**
  - Stopwatch 5 Unit 0 Vocabulary 1 (5.0.V1).pdf
  - Stopwatch 5 Unit 0 Vocabulary 2 (5.0.V2).pdf
  - Stopwatch 5 Unit 1 Vocabulary 1 (5.1.V1).pdf
  - Stopwatch 5 Unit 1 Vocabulary 2 (5.1.V2).pdf
  - Stopwatch 5 Unit 2 Vocabulary 1 (5.2.V1).pdf
  - Stopwatch 5 Unit 2 Vocabulary 2 (5.2.V2).pdf
  - Stopwatch 5 Unit 3 Vocabulary 1 (5.3.V1).pdf
  - Stopwatch 5 Unit 3 Vocabulary 2 (5.3.V2).pdf
  - Stopwatch 5 Unit 4 Vocabulary 1 (5.4.V1).pdf
  - Stopwatch 5 Unit 4 Vocabulary 2 (5.4.V2).pdf
  - Stopwatch 5 Unit 5 Vocabulary 1 (5.5.V1).pdf
  - Stopwatch 5 Unit 5 Vocabulary 2 (5.5.V2).pdf
  - Stopwatch 5 Unit 6 Vocabulary 1 (5.6.V1).pdf
  - Stopwatch 5 Unit 6 Vocabulary 2 (5.6.V2).pdf
  - Stopwatch 5 Unit 7 Vocabulary 1 (5.7.V1).pdf
  - Stopwatch 5 Unit 7 Vocabulary 2 (5.7.V2).pdf
  - Stopwatch 5 Unit 8 Vocabulary 1 (5.8.V1).pdf
  - Stopwatch 5 Unit 8 Vocabulary 2 (5.8.V2).pdf
  - Stopwatch 5 Vocabulary Answer Key.pdf

Class Audio CD 1
- Track 1—Track 41

CD 2

- **Project Rubrics**
  - Stopwatch 5 Project Rubrics
- **Scorecard**
  - Stopwatch 5 Scorecard.pdf
- **Test**
  - **Final Test**
    - Stopwatch 5 Answer Key Final Test.pdf
    - Stopwatch 5 Final Test.pdf
  - **Mid-Term Test**
    - Stopwatch 5 Answer Key Mid-Term Test.pdf
    - Stopwatch 5 Mid-Term.pdf
  - **Placement Test**
    - Stopwatch Placement Test Answer Key.pdf
    - Stopwatch Placement Test.pdf
  - **Standard Test**
    - Stopwatch 5 Answer Key Standard Test.pdf
    - Stopwatch 5 Standard Test U1.pdf
    - Stopwatch 5 Standard Test U2.pdf
    - Stopwatch 5 Standard Test U3.pdf
    - Stopwatch 5 Standard Test U4.pdf
    - Stopwatch 5 Standard Test U5.pdf
    - Stopwatch 5 Standard Test U6.pdf
    - Stopwatch 5 Standard Test U7.pdf
    - Stopwatch 5 Standard Test U8.pdf
  - **Test Plus**
    - Stopwatch 5 Answer Key Test Plus.pdf
    - Stopwatch 5 Test Plus U1.pdf
    - Stopwatch 5 Test Plus U2.pdf
    - Stopwatch 5 Test Plus U3.pdf
    - Stopwatch 5 Test Plus U4.pdf
    - Stopwatch 5 Test Plus U5.pdf
    - Stopwatch 5 Test Plus U6.pdf
    - Stopwatch 5 Test Plus U7.pdf
    - Stopwatch 5 Test Plus U8.pdf

Test Audio CD 2
- Track 1—Track 8 Unit Tests
- Track 9 Mid-Term
- Track 10 Final Test

Verb List

Present	Past	Past Participle	Present	Past	Past Participle
bake	baked	baked	pour	poured	poured
bark	barked	barked	put	put	put
be	was / were	been	retire	retired	retired
board	boarded	boarded	ride	rode	ridden
boil	boiled	boiled	roast	roasted	roasted
break	broke	broken	run	ran	run
earn	earned	earned	send	sent	sent
feed	fed	fed	sing	sang	sung
feel	felt	felt	sit	sat	sat
find	found	found	snore	snored	snored
forget	forgot	forgotten	spend	spent	spent
fry	fried	fried	spill	spilled	spilled
grill	grilled	grilled	sponsor	sponsored	sponsored
grow	grew	grown	steal	stole	stolen
hang	hung	hung	steam	steamed	steamed
hold	held	held	sweep	swept	swept
keep	kept	kept	think	thought	thought
know	knew	known	throw	threw	thrown
learn	learned / learnt	learned / learnt	understand	understood	understood
leave	left	left	wear	wore	worn
lose	lost	lost	wipe	wiped	wiped
meet	met	met	write	wrote	written

Phrasal Verbs

break up: to end a relationship

clean *sth out: to make a place clean by removing all the objects that you don't need

clean *sth up: to make a place completely clean, especially if it is dirty

figure *sth out: to solve a problem or find an answer

get along with: to be friends with someone

get over: to recover from a bad experience

give *sth up: to stop doing something

go on: to continue doing

hang *sth up: to put clothes on a coat hanger and put them in a closet

keep *sth to (myself): not to share some information with other people

own up: to confess you did a crime or broke a rule

pick *sth up (1): to clean and tidy a room, especially a bedroom

pick *sth up (2): to collect your luggage after you get off a plane

put *sth away: to place an object inside a closet, desk, etc. after you use it

take *sth out: to move something out of a house, building or room

tell on **so: to report someone to a parent or teacher for breaking a rule

throw *sth away: to put something in the trash because you don't need it

turn **so in: to report a criminal to the police

wipe *sth off: to clean a dirty surface with a wet cloth

* something   ** someone